Channelling
for
Everyone

TONY NEATE

Channelling for Everyone

A SAFE, STEP~BY~STEP GUIDE TO
DEVELOPING YOUR INTUITION
AND PSYCHIC AWARENESS

PIATKUS

To Ann
whose patience and encouragement
are always there

© 1997 Tony Neate

First published in 1997 by
Judy Piatkus (Publishers) Ltd
5 Windmill Street, London W1P 1HF
www.piatkus.co.uk

Reprinted 1998 (twice), 2000

**The moral right of the author
has been asserted**

*A catalogue record for this book is available
from the British Library*

ISBN 0-7499-1720-2

Edited by Esther Jagger
Designed by Sue Ryall
Artwork by Zena Flax

Set in Baskerville by RCL, Bungay, Suffolk
Printed and bound in Great Britain by
Mackays of Chatham PLC, Chatham, Kent

Contents

Acknowledgements

I would like to thank the following people: H-A, whose inspiration has brought meaning and motivation to my life; Ann, my wife and soulmate, without whom this book would never have been finished – she worked alongside me, improving my English, helping me to get the balance right and spent countless hours dealing with my impatience; Dr Andrew Powell and Gilly Wilmot for contributing the Foreword and Introduction; Susan Mears for her help and guidance; Lorraine Stevens and Gilly Wilmot for reading the first draft; Semira Fardon, my daughter, for typing the manuscript; and Murry Hope, my first wife, who originally introduced me to the world of psychism.

Foreword

Dr Andrew Powell

This book bears all the hallmarks of Tony Neate's personal character: down-to-earth, humorous and full of common sense. At the same time, it is deeply concerned with his commitment to the spiritual dimension of life and with the far-reaching implications of this awareness.

I first met Tony some ten years ago at a talk he was giving. I was struck by his openness, vitality and thoughtful concern to communicate his experiences in the field of healing to an audience of mental health professionals likely to be sceptical at best and adversely prejudiced at worst. He succeeded, I think, because he spoke simply, with intelligence and sincerity, and having no need to impress. His account of working in the transpersonal domain and with subtle energies, intrigued me.

From a clinical standpoint, I found myself calling to mind patients whose problems did not fit well into the psychoanalytical framework, which had been my own therapeutic background. Then there were other patients I had puzzled over, those who had heard voices, or experienced religious mystical revelations, but who did not show the gamut of symptoms which, taken together, leads to the diagnosis of schizophrenia. And what about others suffering from emotional hypersensitivity and who had coped by means of detachment, but at the cost of depersonalisation, including going 'out of body'? In recent years, the near death experience too has had to be taken into account. The list goes on, and it must be owned that there are many strange things which from the psychiatrist's perspective refuse to be pigeonholed.

People avoid seeing psychiatrists unless they are deeply in trouble and are breaking down in one way or another. This understandably predisposes the psychiatrist to interpret what is going on as a sign of pathology, requiring intervention and treatment. Very often the patient's suffering is diminished, to everyone's relief. The aim is to return to a safe and familiar world and to put the unhappy episode behind one. This approach is reinforced by the medical model of mental illness which has gone hand in hand with the scientific and cultural expectations of Western society. Advances in biochemistry, along with the new brain-scanning techniques and the undoubted success of certain drug treatments, have all served to highlight the biological basis of a variety of abnormal mental states.

But this is not the whole story and, given the complex emotional nature of humankind, will never be. To take just one familiar metaphor, however much we know about the car, there is the driver to consider. Arising out of this self-evident, subjective truth comes the whole body of psychological theory. We live our lives contributing to, and being shaped by, a world of meaningful interactions which begin with the baby in its mother's arms, indeed pre-natal experience must be included. The unfolding of the human psyche through childhood and beyond is nothing short of a miracle. Small wonder, then, that when the right conditions are not met the emotional wounds which follow are deep and long-lasting.

This is where counselling and psychotherapy come in, whether on their own or in combination with drug therapies. They did not originally find ready acceptance within the scientific community, but over the last fifty years they have been grudgingly accommodated and are now given due weight. So long as the psychiatrist confines himself to the biological and what we might call the psycho-social aspects of the mind, he is on safe ground.

However, there is still much which remains off limits. Spiritual emergencies are outside the range of many psychiatrists who feel uncomfortable when the word 'soul' comes into the conversation. Yet a spiritual crisis can be a turning point in a person's life, when a painful but necessary move forward occurs in ways entirely unforeseen; likewise our concern with bereavement and other traumatic losses, which so often raise fundamental questions about the purpose of life. These are not occasions which in themselves call for the priest or the philosopher. The first person to ask is the patient or client, for his or her own wisdom or 'higher self' is there to be consulted if given the chance.

This kind of work also requires accuracy and discernment. It is often complicated by problems in the psychological sphere and sometimes biological instability as well. But it is not to be glossed over if there is to be any real progress. Healing means wholeness, and wholeness means taking into account all levels of disturbance.

In my own case, the talk which I heard Tony Neate give one winter's night in Reading emboldened me to question the limitations of psychiatry in a new way. I found patients relieved to be able to talk about matters of spirit without having it interpreted as fantasy, and free to talk about loved ones 'on the other side' without fear of being thought mad. I met a good many healers, people having the same exceptional sensitivity as some of my patients but with the difference that they were leading healthy and integrated lives and putting their sensitivity to good use. Last and not least, there are those with the receptive faculty for bringing through energies which will, I think, elude contemporary science a good while yet, just as water cannot be captured in a clenched fist.

At this subtle level, the communication can only be subjective. Validation takes on a new meaning, because it cannot be measured with tools, only by its effect. 'Therefore by their fruits ye shall know them,' taught Jesus. This is why only the highest level of spiritual intent will do. I do not mean that a person needs to be a saint, but in sincerely asking for guidance from the higher self within or, as in the case of H-A, from without, there has to

Foreword

be purity of heart and a genuine wish to learn and grow. Likewise, as Tony Neate makes very clear, information received has to pass the same test of thoughtful scrutiny. Guidance, whatever the source, should never mean handing over responsibility for one's actions. In Chapter 13 of this book, H-A discusses this crucial question with firmness and eloquence.

A flood of books concerned with channelling are now available and, because of the subjective nature of the process, the door is wide open to abuse. This brings me back to the sub-title of this book, 'A safe, step-by-step guide to developing your intuition and psychic awareness'. The chapters of this book do indeed take the reader forward one step at a time, and taking time to reflect on each in turn will repay handsomely. Unobtrusively and without jargon, a substantial amount of down-to-earth psychology finds its way into the pages, interwoven with the spiritual content. The exercises given, many of which draw on the creative power of visualisation, are straightforward, effective and healing in nature. When a cautionary note is sounded, it is with good reason and worthy of attention. The simplicity of the book and the gentle touch with which it is written might tempt the reader to think it lightweight. Not so, for the art is in the telling and truth which is carried lightly in the heart is carried the furthest.

Andrew Powell MRCP, FRCPsych., is a psychiatrist and consultant psychotherapist in the National Health Service.

Introduction

Gilly Wilmot

I am writing this introduction to Tony Neate's book from the perspective of someone who was trained by him and now works alongside him in the School of Channelling. I should like to share some of my perceptions of the process of developing as a channel, and to describe Tony's contribution to my own development.

I want to begin by offering you an idea – the idea of the transformative journey. This idea is an archetype, central to all mythology (for instance, the quest for the Holy Grail), and generally involves the hero/heroine setting out on a quest of deep personal significance. The quest brings difficulties, challenges, tests and trials. The seeker overcomes those and moves closer to the Grail. Though these initiatory experiences are often solitary, help is on the way; it takes the form of signs, omens, guides, teachers and synchronous events. Each encounter brings its own unique learning. The seeker moves further along the path of self-discovery towards his or her place of wisdom and enlightenment.

My own journey into channelling began with a synchronous event. I travelled to Malvern to explore its beautiful hills, and on a high peak I prayed for spiritual direction in my life. I was unaware that Runnings Park, now home of the School of Channelling, lay at the foot of those hills. Not long afterwards I experienced a psychic 'opening up' which led me into a series of intense psychic experiences. Perhaps the most intense of these was automatic writing, which I now realise was the forerunner to verbal channelling. I would suddenly have a strong impulse to begin writing: the words came very fast, but I had no idea of the content until the 'communication' ended. Although much of the material was interesting and sometimes moving, its source was mysterious. I did not feel in control of the process. I was also sceptical about the whole business of psychism.

About four years later I went on a healing course at Runnings Park, and shortly afterwards started working with Tony on a one-to-one basis. His approach to the development of psychic awareness felt immediately right for me. I needed to feel that I could develop my abilities in a safe, contained environment. In order to use my psychic energy effectively I required training and discipline. Like any natural, creative ability, it needs to be harnessed and honed to realise its true potential.

My scepticism must have made me a difficult pupil. I constantly wanted proof that my channelling was real. I tended to be over-analytical and to judge the content as either true or false. Most of all, I was deeply self-critical. Tony was patient, gentle and encouraging; he suggested that I should befriend doubts and fears rather than condemn them. When challenge or confrontation were the way to help my development, Tony did not flinch from them. Like all good teachers, he knew when to give the pupil a push – in my case, important initiatory steps on my channelling journey. At the same time Tony's keen sense of fun ensured that laughter was present in most of our sessions; it lightened the atmosphere and yet grounded me at the same time.

What does it feel like to channel? The nature of mind and its potential has always intrigued me, and when I first began verbal channelling I was aware that I was opening up to a completely new experience. I remember feeling that my body was becoming lighter – a pleasant, relaxed, floating sensation. I was aware of a gentle breeze around me and a slight pressure, usually on the left side of my head; a faint fragrance accompanied the breeze. The silence seemed to deepen, and the atmosphere became very still. There was an impression of something or someone quite tall standing by the side of me: it felt like a masculine presence. I was aware of some words coming into my mind, but the fundamental experience was one of a quality of energy. The feeling of love and peace seemed to envelop me. I was conscious of the words as they came in, but after I returned to my normal waking consciousness I remembered little of them. Unlike the automatic writing, which just involved a stream of words, this process involved me more completely. With time and practice I was able to 'hold' the energy and a flow of communication began. The ideas and language felt very different from my own: whatever I was experiencing was unlike my normal perception. A turning point came when I first brought through H-A, the guide Tony has worked with for many years. I began to work with this guidance, developing a deep love and respect for H-A's gentle wisdom.

Many people have found Tony's guidance a crucial element in their channelling journey, and in due course it became clear to him that a more formalised structure was needed to support people in their quest. So in 1992 Tony and Ben Stevens set up the School of Channelling. Just as Runnings Park was Tony's response to a perceived need – the need for us to acknowledge and develop our sixth sense of awareness – so this book responds to that same need. It helps the reader to understand the fascinating world of channelling, and to embark on a safe journey of development. Each chapter is opened by an apposite quotation from H-A, channelled through Tony. The account of channelling's long and eventful history reminds the reader that every historical era, including our own, presents different challenges and opportunities for those on the road to awareness. As the title indicates, the book tells us that channelling is indeed for everyone: it is an ability that we all possess and can develop if we so choose. Tony ably demystifies the subject, but also stresses its sacred aspects. The book distinguishes clearly between psychism on the one hand and spirituality on the other, and explains the interface between them. It blends the practical and the aspirational.

Tony explains clearly and simply the different subtle aspects of our being. He emphasises the need to keep all these levels in balance while we develop as channels. We learn how we may take charge of our psychic energy and how to use it wisely. An important part of the channelling development is an understanding of the boundaries of the self – the need to return safely after making a journey outside three-dimensional reality. We are encouraged to sail into exciting new waters, but to bring with us our instruments of navigation. The book takes the view that we must be grounded before we can fly. Guidance is given for psychic protection, and the techniques presented are simple and effective. The emphasis is always on self-responsibility.

On a practical level the book gives clear, concise guidance on preparing to channel and taking the first steps. It includes helpful information on what to expect when we start channelling. Drawing on many years of experience, Tony enables the reader to handle doubts and scepticism in a positive way. He describes some of the changes that may come about as a result of channelling, and suggests ways in which to integrate them. The lovely touches of humour throughout the book remind us how important it is to keep our sense of perspective and not become over-serious as channellers.

Finally, let us return to the mythical journey. As seekers we are each travelling to destinations unique to ourselves, but the shared experience lies in the journey, the process which we experience. T. S. Eliot wrote: '. . . and the end of all our exploring will be to arrive where we started and know the place for the first time.' Our quest may take us on a memorable adventure in consciousness, and with this book Tony Neate offers us a trustworthy guide and companion on that adventure.

Gilly Wilmot MCOH is a counsellor and healer.

Author's Prologue

This is a handbook on channelling, which first introduces you to its history and gives you an explanation of what it is about. Then, from Chapter 3 onwards, it will guide you safely, step-by-step, through the knowledge and understanding necessary for inner development of this nature. I have included a number of important exercises which will help you to take the step into channelling with greater assurance and awareness, and make you better equipped to handle contingencies as they arise. With the aid of my instructions you will gradually discover for yourself your own ability to 'let go', allowing the wider states of consciousness to become part of your everyday life.

I must emphasise that you will need to find someone to work with and share progress: doing so makes the process safer and far more satisfying. If you have any doubts or worries, contact one of the organisations listed on p. 153. I also advise you to read the book from cover to cover before starting any of the exercises. Only then should you start to work through it in sequence from Chapter 3.

Chapter 1 describes my own introduction to channelling, and maybe some of my experiences will resonate with you. My account will also show you how much easier it is today to find out about these things and to realise that, if you are prepared to take the plunge, it will broaden your whole life, bringing new dimensions of understanding into the creative aspects of your being.

The book includes comments by my long-time guide H-A. All H-A quotations are channelled through me unless otherwise indicated.

CHAPTER 1

Beginnings

*'You are part of something so vital and meaningful, that you need
to savour every second in your physical incarnation.'*

H-A

My psychic activities began in the early 1950s with an upturned
glass on a table, but the adventure had started long before that. I
had married young, in my twenty-first year: both my first wife,
Murry, and I wanted to leave our homes for different reasons. In
that sense it was a marriage of convenience, although at that
time I had little idea of the extraordinary journey that was to
emerge from the relationship.

Murry was somehow different from other girls whom I had
met. She challenged a feeling of being stuck within myself; even
more important, she stirred a part of my memory that spread
over many lifetimes. I could not identify this feeling as such at the
time, but I do remember being driven forward by some inner
motivation. It felt exciting, as though there was something
important round the next corner, although I didn't know what it
was. It felt scary, risky, but I knew it was a route I had to take,
however painful it might be.

This inner feeling has stayed with me throughout my life. I
was a shy, only child, sensitive to psychic atmospheres and ghosts,
yet desperately anxious to be accepted by my peers as 'normal',
all the while knowing that inside me a seed was growing that
would eventually emerge as being far from 'normal' in the
accepted sense. On the whole I had disliked sport, as it seemed to
be a waste of time: this was encouraged by my not being very
good at it – I could never see a ball accurately! But I did enjoy
running and for a few years in my late teens I rowed. On the

other hand I was certainly not a bookworm, preferring always to live in the moment and to enjoy what I then thought were fantasies in my mind. I think I have always been aware of energies around me and sensitive to their ambience. When I heard about 'guardian angels' and 'personal guides', it made complete sense to me and explained many of the mysteries of my early life.

In fact, when I look back I am amazed at the way I was guided and prepared for what was to happen. For example, because I went to school during the Second World War and was classified as OD (Other Denominations) due to my father being a Methodist, I received no formal religious education and to this day have never read the Bible. I believe that this lack of conventional spiritual teaching has enabled me to channel a philosophy unencumbered to a large extent by the Christian culture into which I was born. However, my early upbringing had been dominated by my father's fear-ridden religious beliefs which led me to become an agnostic, with my personal feeling that, if there was a God of love, he/she couldn't possibly reflect the intolerant and restrictive views of my father! Now I ask – were these his agendas or mine?

Quite soon into our marriage Murry became interested in the paranormal and, together with some friends, started experimenting with an upturned glass on a table. With the knowledge that I have now, I would never recommend anyone to launch into psychism in this way. But we did and we were fortunate, for it led into a new life and understanding for us both.

In the beginning I was fairly sceptical of 'trying to contact spirits on the other side', and was reluctant to join in. But I suppose it was boring to sit out while the others played, so eventually I gave in. Much to my surprise, I felt a tingling when I placed my index finger on the upturned glass. The glass was placed in the middle of the table and around it in a circle were small cards with the letters of the alphabet on them, plus two extra cards bearing the words YES and NO. Suddenly the glass began to move quite rapidly around the circle, and we realised that we were beginning to receive some coherent messages.

One feature I remember well was that whatever was influencing the movements of the glass either liked or disliked you. On one occasion, when someone was sitting at the table whom it disliked, the glass flew off and struck this person fair and square in the chest. The recipient was so shocked that he fell right over the back of his chair!

The next stage was when Murry found out about psychometry: she tried to get me to see things when I held an object that belonged to someone – preferably someone whom I didn't know. At first nothing happened, especially when my logical mind jumped into the breach and assured me that the whole thing was preposterous. After all, I was that normal person I had persuaded myself I wanted to be, and normal people do not practise psychometry. But Murry prevailed, and I gave in and had another go. 'Imagine a TV screen in your mind and that you are turning the set on,' Murry suggested. Lo and behold, I saw a picture and described what I saw – to the delight of those present. I soon found that these 'pictures' made sense to the owner of the object.

This was to be the beginning of a new era of my life, for it quickly became a fascinating hobby, filling every evening; and no one was more amazed than I was at the considerable accuracy I seemed to achieve. I found myself doing the readings for friends and for friends of friends, all the time trying to make it more difficult by asking them to provide objects that gave no clue to either the identity or sex of the owner. Even I was amazed at the high percentage of readings that appeared to be 'on target' and were sometimes of actual help.

Here I must emphasise that, at that time, there was nothing spiritual in my motivation – just curiosity. What did all this mean?

My next discovery took place when I gave a reading for the owner of a fine pair of earrings, who told me that my comments made no sense whatsoever. I tuned in again and received the same quite clear indications. Had I done something wrong, or had it not worked this time? As I held the earrings a little longer, I intuitively knew that they had belonged to someone else quite recently. When the reading was passed on to the previous owner (the earrings had been given by a mother to her daughter a few months before they were brought to me), it fitted perfectly. This experience enabled me to begin to see how psychic energy works.

Then one evening, as I was sitting in the kitchen of our flat in South London giving a reading, I had my first trance. I felt a build-up of energy around my head, was aware of the presence of someone near me and then thought I had fallen asleep. But I hadn't. 'Someone has been speaking through you!' I was told when I next opened my eyes. I had been in trance for an hour.

Those early days were really exciting – it felt like discovering the wheel! We met frequently, curious to see what would happen next. One evening, I remember picking up a spirit who claimed to be Sigmund Freud. He was very Germanic and very precise. He even quoted from a book he had written, and we were able to verify the information by checking it out at the Westminster Library. The section quoted, including the page number and so on, was exactly as given, *but in German*. A translator helped out, and the contents of the message were discovered to be 100 per cent accurate.

Another spirit, claiming to be the famous Australian singer Dame Nellie Melba, came through, telling us about a performance she had once given in Brussels. This was checked and found to be true. She also helped Murry, who had trained at the Royal College of Music, with some technical singing advice. On one occasion, I was approached by a friend who was in a London show and wished to escape from a one-way theatrical contract – one in which the show management can terminate your employment at any time, but you cannot give your notice to quit until the end of the show. I brought through a departed spirit who claimed that he had been a French lawyer named René

Taillard. He advised very firmly on a course of action that needed to be taken. His advice was followed and the person concerned was able to leave the show without any repercussions – a considerable achievement that required specialist legal knowledge.

Being able to help people in this way felt very rewarding and I began to wonder what would happen next, for I have always been curious to know what lies beyond the next corner. You could say that it has been my philosophy, one which I believe has led me to many riches in my life, often of an unexpected nature. Looking back, the really fascinating aspect of all this was that I had another life, for my principal occupation was working as an accountant for a large oil company. At that time, matters psychic were still very much frowned upon – it was only in 1951 that the Witchcraft Act was finally repealed! And so I found myself living two lives. I didn't find that at all easy, although with hindsight I realise that it was my *practical* job that helped me to keep grounded.

This double life had its hair-raising moments. I can remember on one occasion being featured on a middle-page spread in a Sunday tabloid and being quite terrified at the possible response when I turned up for work on the Monday morning. In the event no one even referred to it, although there was one amusing out-come at a later date when I attended a staff cocktail party. I was approached by one of the directors of the company, who asked me to read his hand! Unfortunately, I never found out whether he was also psychic and recognised me as such, whether he had read the article or was merely a little drunk. It might have been all three!

Events moved on and one day, when I was doing a trance 'sitting', I became aware that there was a Native American guide overshadowing me. I challenged him, and felt him beginning to merge with my consciousness. This was to be an important event, for it was the first time that I had brought through guid-ance that was philosophical rather than practical. He introduced himself as White Cloud, saying through me 'I am here as a forerunner to someone else who will come and bring a teaching that will challenge existing spiritual concepts.'

For the first time, my curiosity felt out of control. The growth-of-awareness part was fine, and helping others felt fine; but the sudden possibility of some kind of spiritual involvement felt decidedly uncomfortable. This brought back the childhood memories of my father and his dogmatic view of God and Christianity. I can remember an occasion when he shouted at my mother because she dropped a spoon while he was listening to a service on the radio, telling her she would be eternally condemned for her actions! Even by today's standards that was abusive behaviour. So when I heard this announcement of 'someone else' coming who would bring a spiritual teaching, it left me feeling confused and angry and decidedly unworthy. However, it was to be, and my insatiable curiosity overcame my resentment enough to allow me to continue.

I well remember my first impressions of H-A, the guide who still channels through me today and has supported me for so many years. When he first appeared, it was very personal. I saw him as a very tall person, slim and with aquiline features. He had fair, shoulder-length hair parted in the middle and large, slanted, very blue eyes, golden skin and high cheekbones. He wore a long white robe with a blue cloak and golden sandals. Above all I was conscious of the light he emanated – a feeling of immense energy, yet a tremendous sense of calm and justice; he appeared to give out a complete humility. It was as though H-A belonged not to this planet, but somehow to the universe as a whole. Right from the beginning he taught us not only to challenge him, but to challenge any spirit that chooses to communicate through a channel. 'If we are who we say we are, we will welcome the challenge. If we are not, then we will soon disappear, being unable to meet the challenge being offered.' Today I am still aware of his incredible presence, but it is now less personal and much more concerned with the accessing of a finer level of consciousness.

One of the first questions that those who were present asked of H-A was, 'Who are you?' He replied,

'*I am what I am, no more no less.* I am part of the universal
divinity, as you are part of the universal divinity. I see the same
truth as you see, but perhaps I see it in a slightly broader
perspective. If I could convey to you accurately the picture as I
see it, then you would be where I am, beyond the need of all
the self-discovery that you are going through at the present
time. No man in a physical shell can truly know what lies
beyond that which he is capable of understanding at any one
time. And yet that which he is capable of understanding at
any one time can change in itself. Today he will understand
what he did not understand yesterday.

That is who I am. That is where I am and how I am. I am
love, I am light. But are we not all love and light? I am that
which I hope can help you to discover a little more light within
yourselves. If I can help you to discover that light, then we are
both enlightened. For as you benefit and learn I benefit and
learn. I have come from beyond the confines of the planet
Earth to try to help it in its present stage of evolution. I am
part of Earth in its present stage of evolution. It is a difficult
question you ask, for I can only truly answer that if you could
see the question and answer as I do, then you would not be
asking the question. I am not attempting to play spiritual
conundrums with you, but you must accept that I want to give
you an answer that has sufficient depth for you to understand,
without first of all trying to see me as I am not, or making me
what you would like me to be.'

H-A

H-A felt that the *substance* of a channelling was more important
than the name behind the message, and said that if we needed
something to know him by, he could be called Helio-
Arcanophus, meaning High Priest of the Sun. He explained that
this was a title by which he was known when incarnate on the
continent of Atlantis. As the name was rather a mouthful, it soon
got shortened to H-A!

He began to channel his own unique form of guidance

through me, and even in those early days said appropriately, 'Fear is *not* of God, it is of the anti-God.' He spoke firmly about the need to move beyond some of the more restrictive and negative qualities of the previous era, with its need for control, revenge and retribution, into a new era emphasising the positive attributes of self-responsibility and self-empowerment.

I also began to be aware of the changing face of psychism. It was moving away from physical mediumship and the traditional approach of deep trance to a more liberal concept that underpinned the need for personal responsibility in psychism, which could be developed as a means of helping spiritually. Thus we began to herald the approach of *channelling*. This was to differ from the teachings of White Eagle and Silver Birch, two well-known spirit guides of the forties and fifties, in that it would provide a new approach to psychism that was available to all and not just to those who were able to develop as trance mediums.

In the following years, I was to channel H-A regularly. And in the many sessions that took place a philosophy emerged that was to teach our group about meditation, healing, psychic protection and an understanding of the universe. In April 1957, a society called the Atlanteans was formed to study the H-A teachings. We ran small public meetings, in Kensington in West London, at which I sometimes channelled; and during the late fifties and the sixties we even used Caxton Hall in Westminster several times – on one occasion our meeting was attended by some four hundred people. When I look back at those early days now, I think how daring we were. Such was the enthusiasm of youth!

This society was to grow and continue until the late eighties, when all concerned felt that they had moved beyond the need for a specialised group. In the meantime, the impetus created by the society had brought together the group of friends who were to found Runnings Park in 1981, and the members of the society became the nucleus of our present Friends of Runnings Park.

My second wife Ann and I, together with three other families, were co-founders of this experiment in community living; again, a daring venture which has certainly been through many ups and downs. But when we look at Runnings Park today, now a centre for health, healing and self-development, with a lively hustle of activity and many people walking through our doors, we experience a sense of fulfilment and even excitement. H-A's philosophy and all that has sprung from it has blossomed and we feel that its time has come. It is no longer avant-garde. In fact our College of Healing teaching, which we started in 1983, has, at the time of writing, been accepted by the Open College Network nationally at levels 1, 2 and 3.

The psychic and self-development workshops that we originally ran in various venues under the auspices of the early society and, later, the Wrekin Trust (one of Britain's first adult spiritual educational organisations), we have been able to concentrate here at Runnings Park for the past fifteen years in an atmosphere of peace and seclusion on the west side of the Malvern Hills. The School of Channelling (see p. 151) developed naturally from this background as interest and demand grew, and came into being in 1992. One of my first experiences of training was in industry and this showed me how a planned, structured approach could provide a sound basis for teaching. That training has been invaluable to me, and I have adopted these principles in the workshops and courses in self-development and channelling which I have run.

What has channelling done for me? As a person, it has widened my horizons of thinking and experiencing, enabling me, through being in touch with the finer levels of my being, to appreciate and become more aware of the needs of other people, of other forms of evolution and of the planet itself.

In addition to channelling I provide healing, counselling and nutritional advice. In my work as a therapist, the development of my intuition enables me to be acutely aware of my client's condition and the underlying cause of the problem. Being able to see their aura and possible imbalances in their psyche gives me valuable information to help them in their healing process and the way in which I give them healing.

As a counsellor, I often receive insights, clairvoyantly and/or clairaudiently (see Chapter 4), which can enable me to provide support on a much deeper level. The difficulty which sometimes faces me is that I have to hold information about my client that, for obvious reasons, I am unable to share – but that difficulty is small compared to the invaluable help I am receiving on a psychic level. In the field of nutrition, I am again often helped in the quest to determine the underlying causes of the client's condition.

The motivation that has shaped my life must have always been within me, but channelling has certainly enabled me to make quantum leaps in my understanding of life on Earth. At times, I am still astonished by the content of what comes through. Writing this book has given me the opportunity to bring together a lifetime of experiences in the world of channelling and psychic development, and to offer it to be used to open up new opportunities for you, the reader. I hope you enjoy it.

CHAPTER 2

The History
of Channelling

'History is there to be learned from and not lived to.'

H-A

How It Began

There is nothing new in channelling, except perhaps for the word itself. Throughout recorded history there have been many instances of this process, a means by which humankind has sought communication and inspiration from beyond the physical plane of existence. Those who have practised this process, consciously or unconsciously, have appeared under many names – mediums, seers, shamans, mystics, prophets, gurus and so on. Going back into early history, there are thousands of documented incidents of channelling among primitive peoples of all continents and races.

Ancient Egypt and Greece

In the five thousand years that preceded the Christian calendar, the Egyptian culture succeeded the earlier Atlantean archetypal culture and brought forward many of its occult and psychic practices, incorporating them into its own approach to religion and ritual. The 18th dynasty Pharaoh Akhnaton (Amenhotep IV), who ruled from 1378 BC to 1362 BC, was probably one of the greatest of the Egyptian channellers and visionaries and was certainly one of the earliest proponents of monotheism, the belief in one God. An ardent pacifist, he was eventually defeated

11

by his own ideals when he refused to give military support to the Syrians in the north and was assassinated. His inspiration has re-emerged through a number of channellers and he has spoken through me in the early days of H-A. H-A has always been concerned with philosophy, whereas Akhnaton was keen to teach our small group about meditation, healing, how to protect ourselves and handle negative energies.

There was a deep interest in medicine and healing in Ancient Egypt and one pharaoh, Atothis, wrote a book on anatomy in about 3000 BC. The Egyptians used quite advanced surgical techniques, together with herbs and even, it is believed, therapies such as reflexology. Drawings have been found in the Physician's Tomb at Saqqara which show that the therapeutic benefits of manipulating specific points on the feet were already known in Egypt more than four thousand years ago.

The Egyptians believed that the 'afterlife' was similar to life on Earth – even as regards your status. So a priest in life became a priest in death, a poor peasant remained a poor peasant and so on; from a modern viewpoint this all feels a little boring. The Egyptians also developed the concept of 'dream channelling', in which the information is fed to the channeller whilst he or she is dreaming.

During the Ancient Greek civilisation, which extended from approximately 2000 BC to 300 BC, oracles were used to provide another form of channelling, an important part of its unfoldment. Oracles were individuals who would go into trance or an altered state of consciousness in order to access information from guidance beyond normal human consciousness. At Delphi, the site of Greece's most important oracle, the advice of the god Apollo was sought. The pythia, a priestess who went into trance, gave messages that were interpreted by the priests. She sat over a fissure in the ground from which issued herbal aromas which helped her to achieve a trance state. It is recorded that the pythia would utter words that were not her own, but those of the god who controlled her.

In 540 BC the mathematician and philosopher Pythagoras

was known to hold seances, and used a version of what today we would call a ouija board. In his book *The ESP Reader*, David Knight describes the scenario: 'a mystic table, moving on wheels, glided towards signs, which the philosopher and his pupil Philolaus interpreted to the audience as being revelations supposedly from the unseen world'. Other philosophers were interested, too. In *Republic and Laws* Plato described prophecy as 'the noblest of arts', while Socrates spoke of 'the special gift of heaven'. Like the Egyptians, the Greeks were also involved in dream channelling.

The Piscean Age and Christianity

It was Plato who discovered that the sun moves slowly, in a clockwise direction, through the twelve signs of the zodiac, covering the complete 360 degrees in some twenty-six thousand years. This gave rise to what are known as the solar ages. The yearly standpoint is taken from the position of the sun at the spring equinox on 21 March. So it takes a little more than two thousand years to move through one sign of the zodiac. At the time of Christ the solar age had moved from Aries into Pisces, and today we are again on the cusp of two great ages, moving from Pisces into Aquarius. This movement from one age to another brings an effect of heightened energies as the quality of influence changes, and this is what we are experiencing now.

The Piscean Age heralded the era of Christianity and the concepts of unconditional love and forgiveness taught by Jesus Christ. This was a quantum leap in spiritual understanding, as it led beyond the retributive concepts of an 'eye for an eye and a tooth for a tooth'. Unfortunately, the patriarchal emphasis of the Christian Church encouraged the more hierarchical and authoritarian aspects of this age to dominate; with its need to convert and sometimes condemn the more gentle and spiritual aspects of unconditional love and understanding.

It also begs the question, 'Was not Jesus a channel?' This does of course challenge the view that Jesus was God in human form, and is a subject on which people will argue until doomsday. Nevertheless, the teachings of Jesus can be seen as a remarkable example of what channelling can offer and maybe the evolutionary status of Jesus can be looked at as a separate issue.

The extension of Christianity and the strong control that it maintained through encouraging the fear of God, supported by its crusading armies and the Inquisition, created an energy that prevented thought developing in an open and non-judgemental way. Sadly, many inspired channels who were brave enough to speak out received harsh treatment, as is typified by Joan of Arc. However, despite this persecution some visionaries survived, among them George Fox, born in 1642 in Leicestershire, who founded the Society of Friends or Quakers, and the Swedish scientist Emanuel Swedenborg.

Born in 1688, Swedenborg started to have channelled visions in his mid-fifties and wrote in great detail about life outside the body. He was also quite a remarkable clairvoyant. There is a true story, told in the book *Three Famous Mystics* by W. P. Swainson, that one evening he was with some friends who asked him, as a test, if he would say which of them would die first. After a moment, he replied, 'Olof Olofsohn will die tomorrow morning at forty-five minutes past four.' Olof was found dead the next morning in his room, where the clock had stopped at 4.45. Swedenborg forecast the end of the Christian Church in its present form and was famous for his studies in physics, mineralogy, anatomy, psychology and spiritualism.

During the same period, in the USA, a man named Joseph Smith channelled material from an angel named Moroni. This was to lead to the creation of the Mormon Church.

Spiritualism

The nineteenth century saw the rise of spiritualism, which has tended to emphasise the personal aspects of channelling and proof of survival, providing solace for those who have recently lost loved ones. Modern spiritualism is a religion and is reflected in spiritualist churches all over the world; some of them follow a Christian tradition and some a wider belief in other masters or avatars. In 1888 Madame Blavatsky, who founded the Theosophical Society, published her now famous book *The Secret Doctrine*. She described herself as the recipient of thought transference from more evolved spirits, either incarnate or disincarnate. In 1 1 Alice Bailey, whose channelled work was and still is published by the Lucis Trust, first encountered The Tibetan, who started to give a teaching supporting what he had previously expounded through Madame Blavatsky. Bailey once said, 'I do not always understand what is given. I do not always agree. But I record it all honestly.' I consider this to be an important feature if one is channelling with integrity. In my own case, I have not always agreed with or understood what H-A has channelled through me, but I have not stopped its publication. An interesting feature of both the Blavatsky and the Bailey teachings was the idea of a spiritual hierarchy and the seven planes of existence. Both these teachings are of the traditional, structured approach to the spiritual path.

Throughout the ages, mankind has been fascinated by the supernatural; there has always been the need to try and prove that it exists. During the last century, spiritualism developed into a religion, exploring the process of communicating with lost souls; and for many people it provided a kind of support system when they lost loved ones. Looking at some of these messages it is possible to see how they are bridging between two levels of consciousness. As we enter the Aquarian Age, interestingly an age of the mind, psychism is moving into a different phase and that transition is already taking place. It will be allied to humankind's ability to understand and use the imaginative, creative, intuitive side of its being.

H-A

Some Other Important Spiritual Channels in the Twentieth Century

No short history of channelling would be complete without mention of the Austrian philosopher Rudolf Steiner, who left a significant imprint on education with the hundreds of schools throughout the world based on his concepts. Steiner also had some interesting advice to give about channelling. In his book *Knowledge of the Higher Worlds and Its Attainment*, he said: 'Persevere in silent inner seclusion; close the senses to all that they brought you before your training; reduce to absolute immobility all the thoughts which, according to your previous habits, surged within you; become quite still and silent within, wait in patience, and then the higher worlds will begin to fashion and perfect the organs of sight and hearing in your soul and spirit.' He encouraged the development of the imagination and of the child as a whole person, including the spirit. Nearer to the present time there was Grace Cooke, who brought through the White Eagle teachings; Maurice Barbanell, who channelled Silver Birch; Ronald Beesley, a man ahead of his time, who in the 1960s channelled dialogue on ecology, education, drugs, psychology and the evolution of consciousness. The philosophy of Ronald Beesley has been brought together by an organisation called the White Lodge. And of course there was the famous American psychic Edgar Cayce, born in 1877, about whom over thirty books have been written. A library in Virginia Beach, Virginia, contains 14,246 copies of his psychic readings. As a psychic, he was well known as a medical diagnostician and as a prophet.

Other Forms of Channelling in History

The concept of channelling goes beyond the areas of spiritual and esoteric teachings to include all forms of inspired creativity: art, music, literature, sculpture, architecture, science, inventions and even politics. Let us look at a few famous names in history.

In the field of music, Mozart wrote a sonata when he was four and an opera when he was seven. In my opinion, he is a typical example of someone who was so open psychically that he found it difficult to be in control of his life. This is one of my reasons for writing this book – to provide basic guidelines on how to maximise, yet control, this creative aspect of our being.

In the world of science, Albert Einstein wrote in a letter to a colleague: 'Quantum mechanics is certainly improving. but an *inner voice* tells me that it is not yet the real thing. The theory says a lot, but does not really bring us any closer to the secret of the "old one" (Einstein's half-joking term for God). I, at any rate, am convinced that He is not playing at dice.' The italics are mine. Other people who, in my opinion, contacted their inner wisdom were Alexander Fleming, who discovered penicillin and Graham Bell, who invented the telephone. Similarly inspired was the political wisdom of Sir Winston Churchill; in art and sculpture, Michelangelo and Leonardo da Vinci; in literature, William Shakespeare. The list is endless.

As this book unfolds, I hope that you will be able to share with me the conviction that, whilst we may not all be geniuses, we are all capable of developing our creativity and inspiration.

CHAPTER 3

What Is
Channelling Today?

*'The purpose of any channelling is not to tell or to instruct, but to
stimulate – to create new depths and new areas of thinking.'*

H-A

Channelling is an extension of our awareness. In our physical
being, we have five senses: those of touch, taste, smell, hearing
and seeing. Beyond that, we have a sixth sense of awareness – an
awareness of subtler dimensions. This is a faculty that everyone
possesses; some people are naturally conscious of it, while others
find it difficult. This sense of awareness manifests in us as either
a yang, outflowing energy or a yin, inflowing energy. And to
understand how this works, we need to look at the functions of
the two halves of the brain, or left and right hemispheres.

Left and Right Brain

Scientists have shown that the left brain differs from but is con-
nected with the right. The first indications that the two hemispheres did rather different things came from cases of brain
injury and brain surgery in the late nineteenth and early twen-
tieth centuries. It became especially evident when the link
between the two halves was broken or when one half was put out
of action, such as in patients who had suffered seizures and other
neurological problems.

It was through the work of neurophysiologists such as Dr
R. W. Sperry and Dr M. S. Gayzonrija that it was finally realised

that the left and right hemispheres of the brain have distinctive functions. Dr Herbert Benson explains in his book *The Maximum Mind* that the left side of the brain sifts and categorises information while the right side serves as a centre for many of our intuitive and creative mental functions. I would like to take it one stage further, beyond Benson, and suggest that the *left* brain not only governs the logical, analytical process, but also the 'doing' and more conscious aspects of the brain and is expressed through the *right* side of our body. Conversely, the *right* brain governs imagery and imagination, receptivity, the wholistic and unconscious aspects of ourselves and is expressed through the *left* side of the body. In the technological age we have tended to concentrate on left brain activity and place less emphasis on, even suppress, the equally important imaginative and creative side. But to function as balanced, creative, integrated beings we need both aspects to work together, complementing each other.

The Sixth Sense

It is the right brain function that is involved in our sixth sense of awareness and manifests in each of us as predominantly a yin (receptive) or a yang (outward) energy. It can be developed and manifest in a variety of ways. The diagram overleaf illustrates how both the yin and yang aspects can develop.

This concept of yin and yang energy was introduced to me by H-A, and I have been fascinated to observe over the years and from experience in many workshops how accurate the idea is. I have found that many people wishing to develop their latent psychic energies have been really helped by being presented with this concept, and indeed by being shown the diagram. Because of the greater emphasis on logical detail in this scientific era, many people have a very undeveloped yin aspect to their psyche; as a result they miss out on a faculty that can be enormously helpful, whatever their chosen path. This book is intended to help those who wish to develop the yin aspect of this energy.

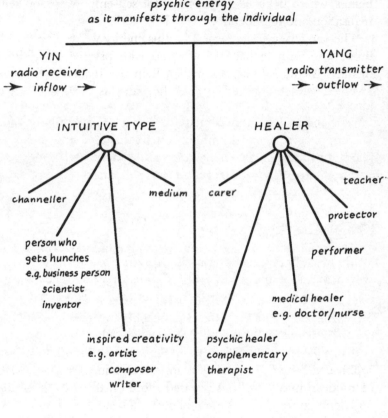

The yin and yang aspects of
psychic energy
as it manifests through the individual

YIN
radio receiver
→ inflow →

YANG
radio transmitter
→ outflow →

INTUITIVE TYPE

HEALER

channeller

medium

carer

teacher

protector

person who
gets hunches
e.g. business person
scientist
inventor

performer

medical healer
e.g. doctor/nurse

inspired creativity
e.g. artist
composer
writer

psychic healer
complementary
therapy

Vulnerabilities

Ungrounded

Blinkered

Most people are predominantly either yin or yang psychically

For many it may feel like sailing in uncharted seas, with an opening up of the psyche which can be immensely fulfilling. It will widen horizons and offer undreamed of dimensions of experience, stretching the mind with new ideas and concepts. I believe it also enables us to become more aware of ourselves as whole beings, which helps us in our quest for self-empowerment, self-realisation and fulfilment.

The yang, outflowing aspect of this energy will resonate with those who wish to become involved with psychic or spiritual healing. In the longer term it will help the reader to become involved with both the yin and the yang aspects, since each balances and complements the other.

Basically, channelling is about allowing yourself to become aware of your intuitive self and extending that intuitive self to become sensitive to subtler levels of consciousness within. So, in whatever creative activity you are involved, you become aware of that sensitivity more acutely. Channelling can also extend beyond this to reaching out on to finer levels of consciousness.

Channelling, then, either comes from the hidden resources of our own unconscious mind drawing on the higher aspects of the self, or it extends further to provide communication through the human mind from a source that exists on a finer and broader dimension of reality than the channeller. Thus some people use channelling in a creative and intuitive sense, while others use it to enhance their spirituality and may choose to channel philosophical teachings. In my own instance, it introduced a form of modern mysticism that is based more on the growth of the individual in freedom than on following a historical master.

However, it is a journey that needs to be undertaken with personal responsibility and care. The development of this intuitive/psychic side of oneself is rather like crossing a busy main road – it's perfectly safe provided you know your Highway Code and look both ways. You need to be aware of what you are doing and follow certain basic ground rules. Tackle it blindly and it will be like crossing that busy main road with your eyes closed.

Not even asking for divine help may save you from ending up like a squashed hedgehog!

From the Piscean Age to the Aquarian Age

There is nothing new in channelling in the sense that it has occurred throughout history, as explained in Chapter 2, yet its present accessibility to everyone reflects the change in psychism that has come about as we transit from the Piscean to the Aquarian Age, the so-called New Age. At different periods in time, the emphasis on psychic awareness varies. Indeed, earlier this century physical mediumship was held to be the last word in proving survival. Today the emphasis has shifted and, as we move closer to this change of influence, the effects of that new influence are beginning to be felt. The Aquarian Age is an age of the mind, and channelling reflects this trend: it is psychism on a mental as opposed to a physical/emotional level. The computer is a typical example of Aquarian consciousness which expands the logical, left side of the brain; but the danger is that it can inhibit the imagination and, on a psychological level, the emotions. We have to be wary that the pendulum does not swing too far in the opposite direction. I believe that this real shift into an age of the mind is also providing the need for a deeper self-awareness of who and what one is.

How Can Channelling Be Assessed?

I am often asked, 'How does one judge or assess channelling?' when it is offering philosophical or spiritual advice. I suppose a quick answer is – with difficulty! This is because each channeller is individual, unique, and offers a different bite of the universal apple. However, some simple criteria are that it should be unconditional in its advice, non-judgemental in its approach, non-manipulative in its attitude, acknowledging human vulnerability and always validating itself with humility.

Sometimes people claim to channel famous historical teachers, mythological figures and so on. May I say, tongue in cheek, that if all the people who claim to channel Jesus are really doing so, he must be a very busy man!

But, since we have mentioned him, let us take Jesus as an example. Firstly, Jesus was a man who died nearly two thousand years ago. However, Jesus the man was able to bring to this planet the wisdom of the Christ level of consciousness, a frequency of energy which is archetypal and accessible to everyone, according to each individual's level of perception. There are also many other levels of archetypal energy: Atlantean, Egyptian, Greek, to name but a few. Sometimes they can relate to the guidance around our planet itself, so we hear of people saying that they are channelling Michael, or Mikaal, the angelic guardian of planet Earth.

If you feel you are channelling one of these archetypal energies, you have to decide whether it is what it claims to be or whether it is reflecting some inner psychological need within you. The proof of the pudding has to be in the eating and not hiding behind a famous name. Although not every channelling has to be a revelation, if it is supposedly from some higher wisdom it does need to have something substantial to say which moves us further towards our individual empowerment.

The purpose of this chapter is to show that channelling is essentially about the growth of awareness in each one of us – that is what is so exciting and challenging. It is available to each one of us in whatever we do, to help us as individuals to reveal our uniqueness and achieve greater fulfilment – to find a true inner freedom.

'Freedom is a state of mind, not a state of being.'

H-A

CHAPTER 4

Developing
Awareness

'In order to find the God without, we need to find the God within.'

H-A

What Is Psychic Energy?

In Chapter 3 the concepts of yin and yang flows of psychic energy were introduced. I explained how yin relates to the inflowing, intuitive side of our nature and yang to the outflowing, active psychic energy of the healer.

Everyone is psychic and, with practice and guidance, can become aware of how they use their psychic energy. The art is to be able to 'tune in' in a safe and contained way, for energy is available in the universe and how we use it is an integral part of our being.

Energy is neither good nor bad; it is always our intention that determines the result. This is very important, for psychic awareness is often confused with spirituality and they are very different. Psychic energy, rather like electricity, is totally neutral. One does not have to be psychic to be spiritual and, equally one does not have to be spiritual to be psychic. However, being psychically aware can help if one is seeking spiritually – it can provide a valuable tool in one's growth and development.

In the practice of healing, the healer is channelling energy from the universe in an outward flow and it is his/her *motivation* that determines the quality of the energy and whether it heals or harms. So the healer carries a responsibility for the way he or she influences the energy which he or she is channelling.

24

Where the intuitive side of one's being is concerned, there are three basic forms of psychic awareness:

Clairvoyance

This means literally 'clear-seeing', and relates to what the psychic 'sees' on a subtle level. People experience clairvoyance in different ways. I find that sometimes I can actually see a spirit – usually in a form that represents it in a previous incarnation (life). So the spirit of a departed relative may appear as he or she was, in a form that is meaningful and descriptive to the sensitive (channel) and/or the person requesting the communication. This form may be experienced as a particular colour or symbolic image.

Clairvoyance is strictly about what you are able to 'see' in your mind's eye, an impression that appears to be totally visual. In the previous paragraph I mentioned colour. I am always reluctant to attribute a meaning to particular colours, for it depends on the channel and the frequency on which his or her sensitivity works. Different colours can mean different things to different people, so I always advise students to compile their own catalogue of colour references and what they mean to them, based on their own personal experiences.

Clairvoyance can also be symbolic. For example, when tuning in on behalf of someone you may see an animal, and this animal may have a particular significance to you and/or the sitter. If you need specific guidance on this, purchase a set of Medicine Cards which offer a Native American approach to interpretation of the characters and personalities of certain animals and birds. Maybe you perceive crystals or historical/spiritual symbols? Whatever form this takes it may be necessary to seek advice, or else contact your nearest reputable bookshop which sells books on these subjects. The College of Psychic Studies in London has a fine and comprehensive library which may help you in your research (see p. 153).

However, use reference books only to support your own interpretation. Ultimately it is always better to create your own levels of understanding rather than relying on someone else's findings.

Clairaudience

This means literally 'clear-hearing' and relates to what the psychic hears on a subtle level. Sometimes, when 'tuning in' you will hear messages or words or even atmospheric music/sounds that provide guidance. In this or any other form of psychic perception it is important always to challenge and check what you receive. Full instructions for this are given in Chapter 8.

Clairsentience

This means literally 'clear-sensing' and relates to what the psychic 'senses' and 'feels' on a subtle level. This is the most common form of psychic sensitivity and covers any feelings that you may receive when developing your sensitivity. It may provide you with a definite feeling about a person, a building or a situation. As well as checking, it is also important to feel and establish that *you* are in control of your psychic sensitivity. Don't allow these 'feelings' to invade you when not asked for. I would not recommend you to try any of the suggestions made in this book until you have read the whole thing and know how to ensure that you are in charge of the situation.

Your sensitivity will respond in one or more of these three ways. All psychic development is unique and individual, and in this sense there is no 'right' way to develop it – only the way that is right for you. There are no short cuts – be gentle with yourself, and allow it to happen in a natural and relaxed manner.

How Do We React to Psychic Development?

The key to all good psychic development consists of maintaining harmony and balance, keeping in control and staying well

26

grounded. As you become more psychically aware, it is not only your psychic centres that become more active, your whole 'metabolism' quickens as if you are going into a higher gear. You become stronger, yet more vulnerable at the same time. When you first start this form of development it may arouse you sexually, as it activates all levels of yourself. This is quite natural and there is no need to feel concerned about it. On p. 79 I explain how to handle this reaction should it occur.

Growth of awareness is like the evolution of the spirit. We start our beingness as a seed thought that, once the gates have been opened, will continue to grow and expand both the light and shadow aspects of ourselves, our inner nature and our needs. How we respond to this awakening is our choice.

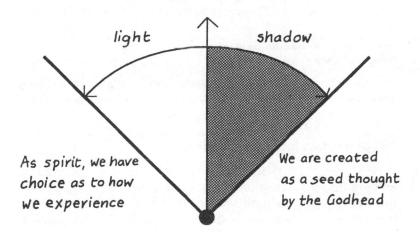

Remember that all psychic awareness is fallible, so we constantly need to question our intentions. Are we doing it to expand spiritually, or to boost our ego?

Different Levels of Channelling

As your sensitivity develops, there is another form of awareness. This is where you actually begin to feel levels of consciousness that appear to be beyond your normal level of understanding. This is a part of our spirit known as the Higher Self. It is the spiritual or divine aspect of our being, connecting us with our spiritual source. As this begins to manifest it will be like clairvoyance, clairaudience and clairsentience all rolled into one! It is a new form of inner guidance that starts to broaden your dimension of thinking and being. Within the new understanding there are three main levels of communication, and the one that will suit you best will fall broadly into one of the following categories:

CONSCIOUS
SEMI-CONSCIOUS
UNCONSCIOUS

Conscious channelling

This is where the channeller is totally aware of what he or she is receiving and has total recall of the content afterwards.

Semi-conscious channelling

This is where the channeller is aware at the time of what is coming through, but retains little or no memory of the content once the session is over.

Unconscious channelling

This is where the channeller is unaware of the content during and after the session, although, of course, his or her mind will have been used for the transmission and there will be an unconscious understanding of the general principles that have been communicated. The last is similar to deep trance mediumship.

In my experience, the validity of the content need not be affected by which level is being used. It is much more important that the channeller follows the route which feels most comfortable.

Some of the Challenges

We need to be aware of the path of delusion, which can be our own self-delusion or delusion from the spirit world.

Self-delusion

As we start to develop that creative and intuitive side, we can easily find ourselves beginning to feel powerful, fooling ourselves with an over-inflated sense of mission, even deluding ourselves that we have come to save the world! As my guide H-A has said:

> 'The moment of finding your importance is the moment of losing it.' I have met many psychics who are so desperately anxious to be right that they forget that they might be wrong. Even if we believe ourselves to be right about something, it is important not to use this to persuade and manipulate others. Only when we rejoin the Godhead, that Ultimate Thought from which we were first created as spirit, do we once more find ourselves in the state of God consciousness, the state of perfect balance and understanding. Along the route, there is no absolute understanding.

Spirit-delusion

When we feel we are receiving communications from the other dimensions, it is important always to challenge the source. As in life, on all other levels of consciousness there are those who would deceive and respond to the desires of your ego, because in doing so it boosts their own.

What Else Do You Need to Be Aware of?

In working in this area of self-development, we need to have a disciplined approach and to be in control. Since we are many-levelled beings, any one aspect of ourselves reflects what is happening on another level. For example, our emotions reflect what we are thinking, and our body reflects our mental attitude. Likewise our psychic state reflects the state of our emotions. If we are psychically blocked or have a psychic problem there will be a corresponding difficulty on an emotional level, and vice versa. So when we embark on a form of channelling development we can sometimes find that a problem starts to surface on an emotional level.

This may necessitate working through personal issues with a counsellor or psychotherapist – preferably one who also understands the psychic realms. Beware of those who are eager to tell you of your past lives, which can be manipulative, misleading and emotionally harmful. On the other hand, past life regression therapy can help to unlock a door. But it must be carried out with an experienced therapist who enables you to produce your own imagery and detail and to make the discoveries yourself.

CHAPTER 5

The Aura
and How to Centre
and Ground Yourself

*'The spiritual quest needs to manifest through
every aspect of your life.'*

H-A

The Aura

Understanding, controlling and being aware of our own aura is
an important step forward in handling our growth of awareness,
and I am suggesting the following exercises to help you to become
aware of and strengthen your aura. You can learn to be in charge
of it, to keep it strong and in balance. You can also learn to deal
with negative energies that may extend from an overbearing,
manipulative person, or difficult energies in the atmosphere that
can accumulate through individual or group negativity.

What is it?

The aura is a 'force field' of energy around each one of us that
helps to keep us integrated. It reflects our state of mind and
emotions and provides our defence against all disturbing influences. If our aura is in balance, then so are we as a whole being.
Everyone can sense this energy field, but will do so in different
ways. It is possible to see, feel, sense, even smell or hear the
resonance of the aura.

31

Furthermore, the aura itself is an invisible radiating field of consciousness which encompasses and penetrates every cell of the physical body. It acts as a protection not only to keep us integrated on all levels, but also to protect us from other energies in the universe – energies that may not be in harmony with our own.

How to sense and understand the aura

The aura is an objective reality, but how one becomes aware of it is a subjective reality. I prefer, therefore, not to define its size, shape, texture or colour. If you become aware of an aura as being egg-shaped – that's fine. If you see it as a kind of mist two or three inches deep, or as a light eighteen inches deep, surrounding the person's body – that's fine. If you see it as a myriad of colours – that's fine. It is as your personal faculties sense it; no one can tell you how it should be seen or felt because you are tuning into it in your own personal way, using your own 'frequency'. However, the aura does reflect the person's emotional and spiritual energy and the state of his/her health. So you could be tuning into one or more of many levels.

The aura not only reflects emotional states, it also, at another level, carries the whole of a person's accumulated experience or karma. In other words, *our aura reflects all that we are and have been.*

If a person comes into life bringing with them unresolved issues from the past – and this applies whether or not one believes in past lives and reincarnation – those issues will provide challenges in this life, to be faced and dealt with. One's spiritual evolution does not begin with physical birth: life as we know it in the physical body is only part of our process. It is who and what we are as a spirit, what we are looking for, that sets the scene for the type of life our spirit wishes to undergo and, hence, the parents we choose before coming into physical being. For example, a difficult life may be chosen by a spirit, in its wisdom, for its own good purpose. It is this innate wisdom and understanding of the spirit that is reflected in the aura.

32

As a practising counsellor and psychic, I have found that my overview of a client's situation as revealed by their aura is much more significant than what they may be expressing in their body language. Whilst there are circumstances in which the client's body language will be consciously or subconsciously manipulated, I have found few cases in which the aura will not reveal the true state of the client's situation. It could only happen if a person was consciously masking their aura.

I am usually able to 'see' auras, and have done so all my life. One interesting discovery for me was that everyone else does not necessarily see them! What is meant by 'seeing'? It certainly is nothing visual; it exists only in the *mind's eye*. I usually see an aura in shades and textures of black and white, with occasional colour if there is a great deal of tension, anger or fear. One thing is for sure – those who can see auras often wish they couldn't, and those who cannot nearly always wish they could!

If you have worn glasses with multifocal lenses, you will know that when you first use them they distort some of the perpendicular images at the side of the lens. But the brain very quickly adjusts the images into what it knows they should be. I believe it is the same type of brain adjustment that takes place when you 'see' an aura. You are actually sensing a set of energy frequencies around the subject which, with patience, your intuitive brain will interpret to provide you with an image.

The resonance of a person's aura is rather like a musical note in that it radiates pulsating frequencies. This radiation can be felt as bands at certain intervals, like higher octaves that can be heard above a sung note. These bands of auric energy radiate with increasing distances between each band, in a kind of geometric progression (see overleaf). With some subjects and some psychics, a band of auric energy further away from the subject may appear more powerful than one near to. I have noticed that when we are giving absent or distant healing, sending healing energy over perhaps thousands of miles, it seems to work better if we can tune in to one of the patient's bands of auric energy.

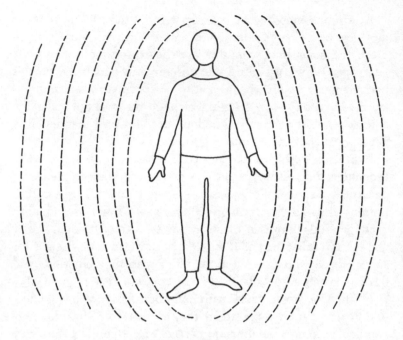

The auric field

Exercise: How to sense the aura

PREPARATION

Find a friend to work with. If you do not know anyone suitable, you could join a group (see list on p. 153) or contact the School of Channelling, which holds a register of addresses of people who may be prepared to practise with you. There may be someone in your area.

Before attempting this or any other exercise, find a room where you will not be disturbed, switch the telephone off and ensure as far as possible that you will not be interrupted by any extraneous noises. Find a comfortable position, either sitting up straight and resting your hands with palms upwards on your knee (which I call the Egyptian position), or in the lotus position (see opposite).

34

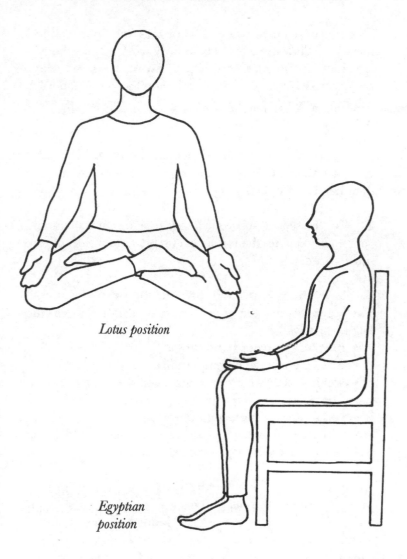

Lotus position

Egyptian position

RELAX YOURSELF

Sit opposite each other and relax your bodies by first of all becoming aware of them. A simple way to do this is to make sure that you are breathing steadily and a little more deeply, in a comfortable way, then to allow yourself to

35

become consciously aware of your toes and your feet: feel them and allow them to relax. Slowly work up your body – legs, hips, abdomen, spine, fingers, hands, arms, shoulders, neck, throat, jaw, tongue, facial muscles and scalp. You will now begin to feel integrated in a relaxed and pleasant way.

1. One of you should stand behind the other. The sitter imagines their auric field flowing and expanding around their head and shoulders.

2. You, the sensor, rub your hands together and then hold your arms out to their full extent on either side of the sitter's head.

3. Slowly move your hands towards the sitter's head until you begin to sense the aura. You may feel or sense in the following ways:
- the palms of your hands tingle
- there is a change in temperature
- you feel as if you are meeting a gentle wall or a sudden breeze
- you sense a perfume or a musical note
- you may actually see the aura, which could be in colour, or you may just vaguely sense it

Do this exercise gently or the sitter may feel a sense of pressure around the head. The way in which you see or sense the aura will be unique and individual to you, and if at this stage you are not aware of any sensations don't worry – just persevere. Your body will gradually become more sensitive to subtle energies if you encourage it.

4. After sensing for about five minutes, stand back and both centre yourselves by focusing your thoughts inwardly and feeling the ground beneath your feet.

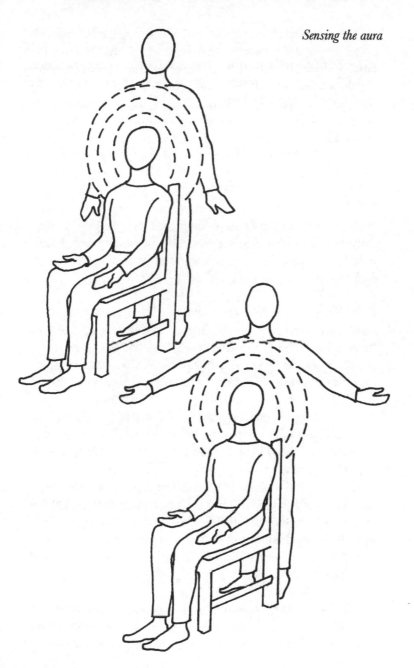

Sensing the aura

5. Now repeat the exercise and ask the sitter to simulate anger for a short period. See what effect this has on the aura. Usually, it will either collapse or seem to explode outwards, according to the person's psychological type.

6. After, say, twenty or thirty seconds, tell the sitter to let go of the simulated anger and place your hands gently on his/her shoulders to reassure and, if necessary, help restore a state of calmness.

7. Now, at the end of the exercise, make sure that you have both 'cut off' any psychic energy that may still be flowing through you. This can be done by brushing your hands together, putting them in cold water or by feeling the energy of Earth beneath your feet.

8. Share your experiences and record them in a journal. If you see the aura in colour, make a note of the detail. See how these colours compare with those which you see in the auras of other people. From these experiences you will begin to understand what different colours mean to you. Many books have been written about auric colours, but in my opinion they tend to represent the personal experience of the author as fact. Psychic perception is uniquely individual and you will need to establish your own set of criteria. This approach applies to whatever way you feel or sense another's aura.

As a general rule, the type of colours that you see in someone else's aura will reflect your own normal associations with various colours. For instance if you regard grey as a generally debilitating colour and you see grey in someone else's aura, this will denote an area of weakness and debilitation in that person.

9. Now repeat the exercise changing places. *Don't worry if you don't sense anything on your first attempt – just try again.* Don't *expect* a particular result – just see what happens for you. If after repeated attempts nothing happens, don't worry. You may be one of those people who needs to join a group (see p. 153 for suggestions).

Important Exercises in Preparation for Channelling

Before you start channelling you need to be properly prepared and the following exercises will help get you to that stage. I talk to many people who are interested in expanding their awareness, and I believe the following exercises will resonate with many readers. In forty-five years of psychic work many ideas have emerged, and in these exercises I have summarised what I have found to be the simplest and most effective ways of safely moving forward. I would like to emphasise that these exercises will help you to optimise your channelling, ensuring that you are in charge, feeling comfortable and enjoying the experiences that lie ahead.

Centring

You need to centre yourself on both a physical and a 'conscious being' level and at the same time become aware of your own auric field which surrounds and radiates from you. In so doing you will not only strengthen your aura and your sense of being in control of yourself and well-earthed, you will also strengthen your psychic protection (see Chapter 8). The Camera Lens and Overhead Projector exercises are particularly effective visualisations to use in everyday situations in normal life, and I have recommended them successfully to many clients. Here are a number of different ways to centre yourself.

Exercise: Focusing

Become aware of the centre of your physical being by focusing on a line of light down the centre of yourself, and feel the air going centrally down into your lungs. Be conscious of a deep stillness within, allowing outer distractions to subside. Repeat three times, slowly and carefully.

Exercise: Connecting Heaven and Earth

Imagine your breath streaming up and down throughout your body, gradually extending down into the Earth and up into the cosmos as you breathe out and in, thus connecting with both cosmic and gravitational energies. Do this exercise three times or until you feel centred.

Exercise: Rooting down

Visualise roots growing down into the Earth from the soles of your feet. If sitting, you can include a third root extending down from the base of your spine into the earth, making a tripod! Again, repeat if necessary.

Exercise: Camera lens

Visualise that you are focusing a camera lens, bringing the picture into sharp focus. That picture is you as a whole person. Remember that in this imagery you are the camera lens as well as the picture, and you are bringing every aspect of your being into balance, harmony and focus. I find this exercise very useful when I need to centre in an emergency. It can be done in a few seconds and can help in many different situations. Try it when you are having to deal with an invasive or disempowering person, who could be a parent or relative, your boss or a colleague at work – in fact anyone who you feel either puts you down, making you feel inferior and unworthy, or overpowers you.

Exercise: Overhead projector

Imagine that you are seated with an overhead projector (OHP) in front of you and that there is a screen in front of it. You have seven transparencies, on each of which is an outline drawing or photograph of yourself in a different colour of the spectrum, red being on top of the pile and violet on the bottom.

1. Switch the OHP on.

2. Place the red transparency on the OHP first, projecting a red outline/photograph on to the screen.

3. Place the orange on top of the red, then follow with the yellow, green, blue, indigo and violet, making sure that each outline sits directly on top of the previous one.

4. Finally check that the transparencies are aligned together perfectly so that only *one* outline remains, which, because it is made up of all the colours of the spectrum, will be *white*.

You have now brought your aura and all your different levels of consciousness into sharp focus. You will feel integrated, harmonious and 'together'. When your aura is in total focus and balance, you will feel in complete charge of yourself and your life.

Sometimes a very psychically sensitive person of yin inclination can find his/her spirit being involuntarily ejected from the body and unable to return in a satisfactory way. This can leave the spirit half in and half out of the body. A sudden shock can be the cause, and the result is that you feel faint and disorientated – 'spaced out' is an apt modern term. It can also make a person feel nauseous, even to the extent of vomiting. Two girls who came to me for healing had had to leave their jobs because they could no longer cope through feeling disorientated. This had been caused, incidentally, by practising an Eastern form of meditation for which they were not equipped.

In most cases, time and the natural self-healing processes of the body will thankfully sort the situation out, but there are simple and effective methods for bringing oneself back into the body.

Exercise: Back in the bottle

I am sure you have seen those TV ads in which the film is reversed and the liquid is seen re-entering the bottle. Imagine that you are the bottle and that the liquid represents your spirit. Reverse the film and visualise all of that liquid going back into the bottle. When the liquid is all in, simply replace the stopper. Repeat three times in order to ensure that all the liquid is in the bottle. Finally, carry out the Camera Lens exercise on p. 40.

Exercise: Cold water

Place your hands in cold water and feel the energy coming down your spine into your hips, and then down your legs into your feet and into the ground.

Exercise: Relax

Do something totally mundane, like having a cup of tea or listening to a party political broadcast!

Exercise: Have fun

Put some lively music on and dance around.

Exercise: Pulling yourself in

Place your hands above your head as in the diagram below, and bring them down your body. As you do so, feel that you are really pulling yourself inside yourself. Finally 'earth' yourself by touching the ground.

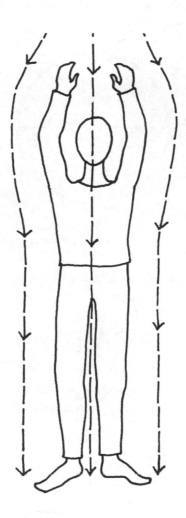

Exercise: Use a symbol

Whenever you centre and harmonise yourself, always complete the process by placing yourself in the centre of a multi-dimensional equidistant cross within a golden sphere. This is a simple and powerful symbol that will also protect you by reflecting back any negative thoughts or energies directed towards you. The meaning of this symbol is explained in Chapter 8.

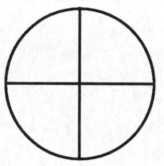

CHAPTER 6

The Spirit,
the Subtle Bodies
and the Chakras

'Evolution is about understanding, not necessarily experiencing.'
H-A

This chapter introduces other subtle aspects of our beings which it is helpful to know about. Once you have understood them they will help keep you focussed and balanced, and thus in a position to channel safely and effectively. A great deal of mystery has surrounded the subject of what are known as the subtle bodies and the chakras. I would like to present them in a simple form and explain what they do. But it is necessary, first of all, to explain how the spirit relates to the physical being.

The Spirit

Our spirit is the innermost part of us, the true essence of our being. It enters the physical body at the moment of conception and leaves at the moment of death. The body which it inhabits provides a physical vehicle for the spirit to experience life on Earth in all its complexity, through the senses, the mind and the emotional aspects of our psyche. We are all aware of these different levels of consciousness that together comprise our whole being, they relate to the energies created by our thinking, our feeling, our sensing, our inner 'knowing' and so on.

45

The spirit does, in fact, motivate the physical body – it is an undetected aspect of ourselves and has a much greater influence than is generally realised. It is the 'thought' behind the 'creation'.

You might wonder how such a fine energy as that of the spirit can influence and express itself through the comparatively dense energy of a physical body. The answer is that the energy is stepped down through a number of levels known as 'subtle bodies' or, more simply, levels of consciousness.

Subtle Bodies or Levels of Consciousness

There are differing viewpoints on the number of subtle bodies that each of us have. What is important is that we understand that they exist and that we work with whichever view makes the best sense to us. As I see it, we are made up of six subtle bodies and the physical body, making seven bodies in all – seven levels of consciousness. Let's now look at the subtle bodies in some detail.

Physical body

Our physical level of consciousness.

Etheric body

This is an etheric counterpart of the physical, sometimes called the etheric double since these two bodies reflect each other. Every physical organ has an etheric counterpart, and when healing takes place it primarily affects and adjusts the etheric body. The etheric then affects and adjusts the physical. So good health depends on the healthy functioning of the etheric body; any malfunction will affect the etheric level first and then translate itself to the physical.

Emotional/astral body

The emotional body carries the feelings which link with both our thoughts and our physical body. We *physically* feel our emotions and can unconsciously develop areas of blocked energy, particularly from unresolved past traumas. They can get stuck in us, so to speak. The emotional body acts as a bridge between the mental body and the etheric and physical bodies.

Mental body

This is the level of our conscious thinking and visualising process which, as we know, can link instantaneously with the emotions. When clear and relaxed, the mental body will allow the finer intuitive energies to filter through.

Intuitional body

This is the bridge between the transpersonal aspects of soul and spirit and the ordinary mental consciousness. Those finer, more spiritual aspects of soul and spirit have greater awareness and understanding, and communicate through the intuitional body via dreams, in meditation and through inspiration. Psychically, this is the level for channelling and the development of the so-called 'third eye' through which we psychically perceive.

Soul

The soul is the aspect of the spirit that incarnates and is involved with our *raison d'être*, what we have come to achieve. It brings forward the motivation of our true essence or spirit into the practical reality of life, helping us to face the karma that we need in order to move forward and evolve, guiding us in our evolution through the choices we make.

Spirit

This is true essence and expression of the divinity that created us. It is partly within and partly without, representing the Higher Self which is our connection with the spiritual source or Godhead.

> 'Matter is spirit at its lowest level.
> Spirit is matter at its highest level.'
> Madame Blavatsky

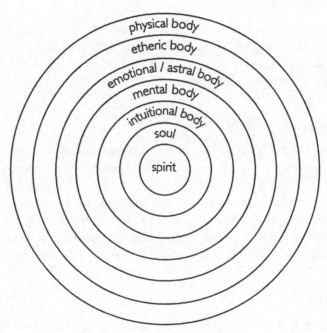

Levels of consciousness/Subtle bodies

The Chakras

All living beings need nourishment, cosmic and spiritual as well as physical. Our chakras connect us with the universe. They are receptive points or, as the psychologist Jung called them,

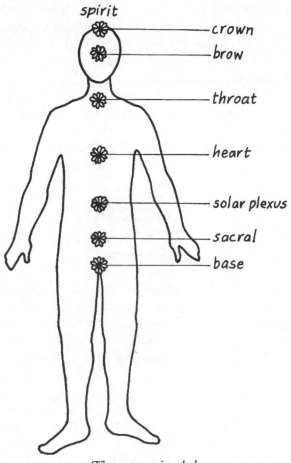

The seven major chakras

'gateways of consciousness' that transform cosmic energies down to the physical level and vice versa. They connect us energetically with the cosmos, enabling us to be physically nurtured by the finer frequencies. Equally, our own thought and feeling processes radiate out through the chakras.

'Chakra' is a Sanskrit word meaning 'wheel', used in this context because the energy appears to spin. These centres or vortices function at intervals down the body, fusing together and linking the subtle bodies, the various levels of consciousness, that make up the whole being. So they connect the many levels within ourselves as well as connecting us as a physical being with the finer frequencies of the universe.

Let's now look at the seven major chakras in some detail. I have included their related gland and the individual colour of the spectrum that correlates with each one, for just as pure light splits into the seven colours of the spectrum, so does the pure light of spirit manifest down through seven levels of consciousness.

Crown
Relates to pineal gland
Colour violet

Opens us up to the source of our being and awareness of the universe and its purpose.

Brow
Relates to pituitary gland
Colour indigo

Governs the intuition, spiritual insight, psychic perception on an intuitive/telepathic level. Idealism and imagination. The gateway to the crown chakra and higher consciousness.

Throat
Relates to thyroid gland
Colour blue

Centre of self-expression and creativity. Opens to spiritual will as opposed to ego-based will. Consciousness of spiritual direction.

Heart
Relates to thymus gland and
*   immune system*
Colour green

Ability to love and care beyond oneself, compassion – especially when this centre is awakened. If this happens before lower centres are in balance, it can cause problems of a physical/sexual nature.

Solar Plexus
Relates to pancreas
Colour yellow

Seat of the emotions and the nervous system. Relates to astral body, physical mediumship, clairvoyance. Any drugs that affect consciousness can make this centre vulnerable.

Sacral
Relates to gonads
Colour orange

Governs reproductive system and sexual activity. Also healing at a cellular level.

Base
Relates to adrenal glands
Colour red

Instinct for survival – 'flight or fight' mechanism. The will-to-be, that draws the physical energy necessary for life.

Balance

The chakras are a total system – no chakra works in isolation. Therefore, on whatever level you might have a problem, the other chakras will also be affected. The exercises starting on p. 53 will balance the whole chakric system. The balance of the chakras can be affected by both over- and under-stimulation of any one particular chakra. For this reason avoid any exercises, however well-intentioned, that promote either state.

Each chakra links with the nervous system via the etheric body. Each chakra also links with the endocrine system through the gland that relates to its particular function. For example, fear, whether real or artificially stimulated by films or other means, draws heavily on the adrenal glands, which connect with the base chakra. With momentary fear, the body easily rebalances itself. But if the fear is prolonged or too frequent, the base chakra will become out of balance and the person will find that their energy is very depleted.

The chakric centres are particularly sensitive to physical and/ or emotional shock, so if you have suffered from either, always rebalance the chakras as indicated in the exercises that follow and in the aura exercises (see p. 39). Our aura reflects the balance of our chakras.

Planetary chakras

All forms of life have an aura, subtle bodies and chakras. Some more traditional schools of thought suggest that more primitive forms of life have only two centres, those of survival and reproduction. I do not personally agree with this view, but feel that there are seven centres in *every* form of life, although in the simpler forms some are undeveloped.

Following on from this, we need to consider the idea that the whole planet as a form of life has a chakric system, subtle bodies and an aura. As above, so below: what the planet is living out, we live out, and what the human race lives out affects the planet as a whole. But also, of course, this applies to every other form of evolution on the planet – the animal kingdoms, the bird and fish kingdoms, the vegetable, flower and tree kingdoms, the mineral kingdoms and so on. So each kingdom is responsible to all the other kingdoms and to the planet as a whole.

Humanity identifies mostly with the three lowest chakras, each person and each nation expressing themselves through the more ego-based, possessive energies and emotions of the personality. The struggle on the planet today is about lifting that energy up to the more altruistic loving and caring qualities of the heart chakra, which is unconditional and embraces the whole. We are beginning to achieve this through our greater awareness of what is happening in the world, through our support of organisations that are really helping those situations, and by developing a more caring community in our own vicinity.

The three higher chakras of throat, brow and crown reflect the finer qualities of soul consciousness which, as our life unfolds and evolves, gradually awaken. Our consciousness opens to spiritual direction expressed by the spirit and soul through the faculty of intuition. So the more influence we can bring to bear from the finer levels of consciousness, the more will our spiritual direction manifest. This is not to assume, however, that we do not need the lower energies. They are equally important in our development as a whole being – indeed, the two lower centres are our storehouses of power, energising all the other centres.

Arriving at a Balanced State

It is the balance of the complete chakric system that is our goal, and a gradual growth of awareness enables that system to function with greater understanding. What path we choose in life, and how we progress along that path, is up to our individual free will. Remember that the more balanced you feel, the more your chakras will be in balance. And the more your chakras are in balance, the more balanced you will feel.

The exercises below will help balance, relax and energise your aura, chakras and subtle bodies. They are simple self-healing visualisations and can be used as often as you wish. As you start to develop your channelling you will discover quite naturally the appropriateness of the different exercises provided in this book.

Exercise: Stroking the aura

Ask your friend/partner to help in this one. Lie down on a bed or on the floor, and get him/her to stroke your aura lightly about six to nine inches above your body, starting at your head and working down to your feet. This will balance, relax and energise your aura.

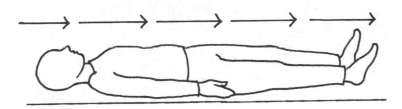

Exercise: Energising and balancing the chakras

Stand up straight. Using your own thought and visualisation, bring energy up from your feet through each chakra to the crown and out through the top of your head, breathing in. Then bring the energy down either side of your body until it reaches to beneath your feet, breathing out. Include arm movements if you wish. Repeat three times.

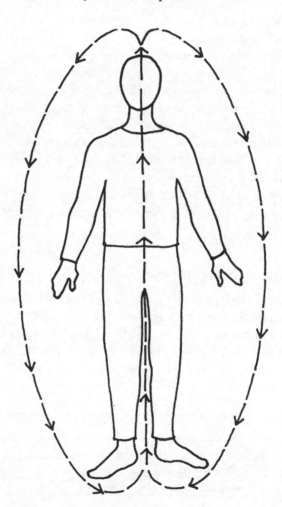

Exercise: Breathing up and down the chakras

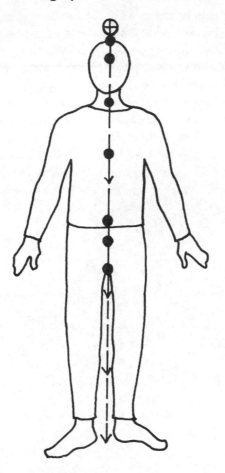

Relax yourself, either sitting or standing, and breathe up and down your chakras, slowly and rhythmically, feeling the energies within balancing and becoming integrated. Extend the thought down to your feet and then beyond, into the Earth, and above your head into the sky. This exercise is similar to the grounding exercise called Connecting Heaven and Earth (see p. 40).

Exercise: Earthing, grounding and protecting

Using the equidistant cross in the circle or sphere as a form of protection (see p. 44), imagine it sitting on top of your head for about five seconds. Then bring it down level with your brow (either inside your head or just in front) for five seconds. Continue in the same way down to the throat, the heart, the solar plexus, the sacral area and the base of your spine. Finally, in your imagination take the symbol down to between your feet for five seconds (there are minor chakras on the insides of the feet). This will help to earth/ground you. Centre yourself and build your aura (see p. 39).

CHAPTER 7

Meditation Can
Help Channelling

*'To evolve, you need to allow yourself to "be", in total acceptance.
If you try to force the pace, it will act against you and impede your
growth.'*

H-A

Meditation has been described as a bridge between inner and outer realities, but also as a bridge to the soul. It can be used effectively to enhance the expansion of your awareness and to provide an important aid to channelling.

Most people meditate without knowing it, as when we go deep into a particular thought. The word 'meditation' has different meanings for different people, ranging from the concept of the Eastern mystic in deep contemplation to the devotional practices of the Westerner.

Above all, meditation is about stilling the mind, disentangling yourself from the environment, the considerations of the ego, finding that true peace within, moving beyond daily life into an altered state of consciousness. It can lead to finding the Higher Self and an awareness of the subtler levels of your being; and it can bring a cognisance of your personal guide (see Chapter 10).

Meditation can also enable you to develop an awareness and control of the mind, body and nervous system that can help every person in ordinary living. You gradually acquire the type of concentration needed to 'collect' yourself physically, mentally and emotionally in times of stress and strain. It can help establish control over pain and anxiety so that, at times of great worry, these symptoms can be put aside temporarily by using a meditational discipline. The spirit can then use this period of respite to communicate to the brain a line of action to overcome the problem.

To summarise, meditation can help you to:

- strengthen your powers of concentration
- gain better access to your memory
- create a stronger link with your Higher Self through relaxation and visualisation exercises
- make contact with your personal guide
- cope with the stress of modern life
- gain a deeper understanding of homo sapiens and its place in the universe
- contribute more positively to your fellow-beings through a more structured approach to your life
- increase your sensitivity to life on all levels and to the hidden dimensions of the universe

Before attempting to meditate, let's look at the different forms of meditation.

Reflective Meditation

This mental process, carried out with eyes open or shut, involves focusing and reflecting on an object, a theme, a word or a thought. For example, the object for meditation could be a flower or a symbol; it could be a thought such as 'My true mind is full of peace', a word such as *love* or *serenity*, or the inner or actual experience of walking in a field and hugging your favourite tree. This is the simplest and safest form of meditation because control of your theme is maintained – you are reflecting on it. It is ideal for those living under the influence of Western culture, where the way of thinking is *active*.

Receptive Meditation

In this form of meditation you hold your mind still and alert to receive inspiration. Unless a strict discipline is observed, involving the use of psychic protection, it can be dangerous as it is similar to preparing to channel. It is more suitable for those living in Eastern cultures, where the thinking and approach to spiritual seeking are more *passive*.

Creative Meditation

Here visualisation is used with creative imagination. The subject or object is observed as before but the imagination extends it, allowing the feeling or emotional nature to become involved. You may experience a plant growing from a seed, a drop of water flowing downstream into the sea, or how it feels to be an animal. This is a fairly safe form of meditation.

Invocation and Prayer

Help is asked for from a higher external force, and so some higher form of consciousness is involved. Again, this is a very safe form of meditation as the higher source is protection in itself.

Exercise: A pattern for reflective meditation

For the beginner reflective meditation is probably the best choice, and a suggested pattern is given below. If you prefer to keep your eyes open during the meditation, rest and relax them for a few moments from time to time.

PREPARATION
Find a comfortable position, either sitting up straight, resting your hands with palms upwards on your knee, or

in the lotus position. Empty your lungs and take a few deep breaths, ensuring that you are breathing deeply. On the 'in' breath extend the abdomen first and then the rib-cage. On the 'out' breath pull in the abdomen first and finally relax the ribs. Repeat a few times. Then relax into a rhythm that is comfortable for you, but a little deeper than normal.

BODY CONSCIOUSNESS
To let go of all physical tension do a 'body consciousness' and relaxation exercise such as the one given on pp. 34–5. Make sure that your aura is balanced and that you are centred.

VISUALISATION
Imagine a fixed object such as a rose, or place one before you. Observe its shape, its colour and texture, its scent (if any), and sense its emanation.

RECOGNITION
Hold the picture, enjoy and admire its beauty. Reflect on its unique qualities – the leaves and stem that support it and the roots through which it is nourished. See the sun reflected in it and recognise it as a symbol of inner growth, unfoldment and expansion.

REFLECTION
Observe the correlation between yourself and the rose – its growth from a cutting into a plant of great beauty with its own roots. Reflect on the growth of *your* inner self, its need to be well rooted in life and its potential to unfold into full bloom.

REALISATION
Realise that *your* soul can unfold and find fulfilment just as the spirit of the rose does.

CLOSING
Close the meditation by grounding or earthing yourself, becoming aware once again of your normal physical existence.

A Few 'Do's and Don'ts'

Meditation is a discipline. It is important to treat it as such and it needs to be practised regularly. But meditation is also an aid to channelling that suits some people more than others. It is not a 'must'. For some people who are yin psychically – in other words, very perceptive – meditation may not be easy, for as they start to relax they will feel tempted to 'wander off' and will find it difficult to remain within the boundaries of the particular meditation. If this is so, it is important to avoid systems of meditation where you are not mentally in control. We live in a society where the spiritual motivation is active rather than passive. So if Westerners choose certain Eastern forms of meditation, however good or valid these may be within their context and ambience, the meditators may have difficulties if they are psychically sensitive – they can quickly feel out of control and 'spaced out'. It is better, therefore, for such people to avoid meditations that involve opening up the consciousness without control, or the sort that uses some form of repetitive affirmations or mantra. These types release auric control, which makes you vulnerable. It may even be necessary to avoid meditation altogether, unless you can meditate with someone who is experienced and who can help rebalance you if you feel spaced out or ungrounded afterwards. Here are some further useful guidelines:

- if you are a beginner, don't try to meditate for too long a period. Fifteen to twenty minutes is more than enough, and for most people first thing in the morning is the best time to do it. Just get up a little earlier!

- don't meditate on a full stomach – you will most likely fall asleep
- never use a mantra or affirmation which you don't understand, or you may find yourself out of control
- avoid any meditation system that offers to inflate the ego, or promises unrealistic goals
- last, but not least, remember the golden rule of all forms of self- and psychic development – *always be in charge of what you are doing. It is your life and your area of self-responsibility*

Further Ways to Grow in Sensitivity

'So when you develop your psychic, your receptive gifts, to be amongst the natural world can be a great help.' This is a sentence from a lecture of H-A's entitled *The Various Forms of Evolution*. As I have said elsewhere, heightening your awareness on one level will encourage other levels to become more sensitive. We are not parcelled out into mind, emotions, body and spirit as though they were four separate parts of a machine. We are *whole* beings, and each of our many levels has a direct effect on all the others.

If our aim in learning to channel is, therefore, to grow in sensitivity, that growth can be greatly enhanced by exercises that help us to become more acutely aware of the natural world around us. It is through our five senses of sight, hearing, taste, touch and smell that we normally connect with that natural world. To actually be there on the grass, leaning against a tree or swimming in a lake is great, but we can also experience all these things without so much as putting a toe outside!

Etheric senses

Developing our inner sight, hearing, taste, touch and smell, is a valuable exercise towards developing our sixth sense. This is something you can do in creative meditation, visualising an inner journey and exercising as many inner etheric senses as you are able.

The elements

As part of planet Earth, a fertile sphere basically made up of four elements – earth, air, water and fire – we human beings also comprise earth, air, water and fire. Each of these elements has a life force within it and, from time to time, it is valuable and healthy to make an inner connection with each of them, honouring the part they play in our bodies and psyches. Here is a meditation which incorporates all these ideas.

Exercise: Visualisation on the elements of earth, air, water and fire, beyond and within

If visualising is difficult for you, sense the scene in whatever way you can.

PREPARATION
Prepare yourself as in the previous meditation (see p. 59) with deep breathing, body consciousness and relaxation. Centre yourself, balance your aura and inwardly smile (this helps the whole body to relax even further).

MEDITATION
Find yourself facing a gate which leads into a field . . . open it and walk into the centre of the field in bare feet . . . through your inner senses, become aware of the colours around you – the greenness and the blue sky . . . hear the sound of birds, or maybe the silence . . . smell the grass . . . feel the earth, firm and stable, beneath your feet, linking your own body with the physical being of planet Earth itself.

Breathe the clear air deeply into your lungs, feeling the connection with all of nature . . . marvel on infinity above you, aware of the infinite possibilities of your own mind and imagination that can focus wherever you will.

Walk to one side of your field where you will hear and see a stream of clear, pure water, bubbling over stones as it descends from its source in the hills beyond. Step into the middle of the stream and feel the water flowing round your ankles . . . marvel at its adaptability as it meets any obstacle . . . turn your mind to any feelings or issues you may have that you wish to let go of and release from your inner world . . . name them one by one and allow them to relax down through your body into your feet and flow out into the stream, to be dissolved and washed away . . . breathe them out.

For a moment consider the wisdom of water in its ability to accept the nature and quality of whatever it meets . . . are you able to accept your own nature, light and shadow? . . . Are you able to accept the nature of others, their light and shadow? . . .

Step out of the stream and lie down on the grass in the sun . . . feel its warmth as it permeates your whole being and drink in its healing energy . . . dwell on the nature of fire for a moment, its power to transform and also its power to destroy if it is not contained and handled well . . . are you able to handle your own inner fire with wisdom? . . .

Return to the centre of the field, remembering your connections with the earth, the air, the water and the fire . . . walk back to the gate and go through it, closing it behind you.

CLOSING

Gently return to where you are sitting or lying. Refocus yourself back into your body, using the Camera Lens exercise or any other grounding exercise from Chapter 4. Feel centred within your auric field.

CHAPTER 8

Psychic Protection and Preparation for Channelling

'The difference between good and evil is intention.'

H-A

This is an essential chapter to read and digest. There will always be those who believe that having faith in some higher deity obviates the need for protection, but in my practice I have met many people who have found out to their cost that we live in an age where individual responsibility is a spiritual necessity.

We need to be aware that there are negative as well as positive aspects of energy, and to learn how to recognise and deal with the negative aspects which can influence and even control us. We need to be in control of our own psyche. In this chapter I am setting out some basic forms of protection that you can use safely at home, so as to be able to handle the types of situation you are likely to meet. However, do not tackle that which you know inside is beyond you. Always seek help and advice if you are in doubt. Some exercises are included, and I consider it vital to do the ones that resonate with you before you embark on any channelling.

The Psychological Implications

If you are having psychic problems they will of course be reflecting problems on a psychological/emotional level, for each level

5

of our being reflects all the other levels. As already explained, we are an integrated whole.

Using any form of protection is not as simple as it sounds, because it involves personal responsibility. For example, I have frequently had to help free a client from a negative influence. It is one thing to clear a person or place of negative energy, but quite another to enable someone to rise above the need for his/her experience. If you don't have good, clear boundaries on all levels, i.e. physical, emotional, mental, psychic and spiritual, you will draw back negative energies to yourself.

In the complexity of life, it is easy to get into a mental and emotional cul-de-sac and remain stuck there; holding on to any negative 'stuckness' will draw negativity on other levels, including the psychic level. The reason why we remain stuck is that to move forward entails risk – it means we must be prepared to challenge those blockages or aspects of ourselves that we have conveniently ignored for so long. It is through facing the fear, for example, that we are enabled to let go of present and past unresolved issues, to rise above that negative experience and move forward.

'How can we deal with fear without being sure that we are not suppressing our fear?'

'By embracing it. It is like the monster in the fairy tales; when ignored, when shut away, it rants and raves and shouts and tries to beat the walls down. When it is allowed to come out, when shown love, understanding and awareness, then that monster has the potential to change and to transform into a being of understanding. The way to tame it, to transform it, is to open the door fully to fear, to absorb that fear, to embrace it, to give it the greatest love, to give it more love than you would give any other aspect of yourself. Then it transforms.

'Fear can be a great teacher. It can reveal to you a need to change, a need to take another direction. By speaking with the "monster", the fear, by allowing a dialogue, you allow for a release of the fear through insight and creativity. I would also like to say that, as well as being the opposite to love, fear is a direct opposite to creativity. It is concerned with nothing growing, nothing moving. It is concerned with stasis, whereas creativity is concerned with movement and growth. If you have a fear and could allow this fear to speak to you at this moment, it might reveal to you an area where you could become more creative, where you could release an important creative aspect of your being.'*

So open the door, my friends, and embrace the fear. See the other side of the mirror – see the reflection of this fear.

H-A (Gilly)

* This refers to a dialogue between the individual and some aspect of themselves (Fritz Perls, *The Gestalt Approach and Eye Witness to Therapy*, Bantam Books).

Different Forms of Protection

Prayer

A prayer is a request for help and reaches up to an appropriate level according to the request. For example, if my prayer is to win the lottery it will be answered from a different level from that to which I would reach if I ask for help for protection from what I believe to be a negative or inappropriate energy. I do believe that all prayers are answered, but in a way that is best from an overall spiritual point of view (which is probably why I haven't won the lottery!).

So when we pray we are not only asking for help from a higher source, we are also opening ourselves to an acknowledgement of what we need to tackle within. This can be a very important first hurdle. I recommend that the prayer is simple and direct, asking for the help that you need.

You can tell negative energies to go

Many years ago I had a female client who felt she had tried everything to get rid of a negative energy, but without any positive response. I realised that her difficulty lay in her inability to be really positive and certain in her intentions; she needed a way to express what she felt that was definite and carried the weight of her feelings and emotions behind it. Feeling that I had tried everything, I suggested to her in desperation, 'Tell it to *piss off!*'

To my amazement, she responded really positively. Her face broke into a smile and, with great emphasis and aplomb, she repeated those words over and over again. When I next saw her, she told me, 'It's worked – I no longer have this problem!' What she had been unable to achieve with gentleness she had achieved with the violence of this particular expression, which had suddenly empowered her.

I believe we have the *right* to tell any influence that we do not need or want around us to go away. It does not have to be done in a sense of revenge, only in the sense of recognising one's own divine source and choice.

'What is negative energy?'

'Everything in the universe has a polarity. Energy is energy and it exists on different frequencies and vibrations throughout the universe. But, like electrical energy, that cosmic universal energy can be used in both a positive and a negative way. So when I refer to negative energy I am actually referring to the shadow, which is the universal opposite to light. As you go forward in your lives you have two choices: you can draw towards you light, you can draw towards you shadow, and your choice reflects your needs and understanding at any one time.

'The type of human emotion that can attract the shadow is principally that of fear, fear that can arise from guilt, from the need for personal power and from the limited concept of crime and punishment that you have on your planet. But it is important to understand that the planet is moving beyond the idea of an eye for an eye and a tooth for a tooth and is moving towards Christ's teaching of forgiveness. And the true meaning of forgiveness is being able to move beyond the need of punishment, because punishment is the opposite polarity to that of crime.

'The greater the punishment, the greater the crime – and you will notice the sequence in which I placed those two phrases. I understand that on this planet you have to regularise the activities of society and this means there have to be rules, regulations and constitutions; but if they become too rigid they create chaos. So I look to the future when, instead of saying, "How can we punish these people or put them away?" we will ask the question, "What caused this person to behave this way? How can we help that person change their attitude so that they no longer need to behave like that?" Of course I understand that there will be those who are not ready to listen, but I cannot emphasise strongly enough the importance of moving towards forgiveness and understanding, and offering to help in a constructive way.

'If you commit a crime you expect to be punished, and in that punishment is the seed for further crime. If you argue that punishment will deter, a deterrent can only be a deterrent through fear, so you are back to square one, for fear will draw further shadow.'

H-A

Mantra

If you are going to use a mantra, a repeated sentence, it is always better to keep it simple. Use something like, 'I am a child of God, please leave me alone.' This will usually provide what you need.

Colour

Once again this is something that is totally individual, but generally there are certain colours that most people find protective. When you feel the need for protection, simply imagine yourself in a bubble of light surrounded by one or more of the three colours white, gold and blue. Let your bubble extend to at least one to two feet around you, above your head and below your feet.

White includes all the colours of the spectrum. It is a very complete colour, generally associated with purity and cleanliness. Blue is associated with the protective feminine and symbolises spiritual love, reflecting the yin principle. Gold represents the sun and is a very positive, strong energy that can be helpful when dealing with disruptive forces. It reflects the yang principle, and when you imagine yourself inside a golden sphere this is a very definitive and secure form of protection, reflecting back any negative thoughts or energies directed towards you. Try each colour in turn until you find the one that feels right for you.

Colour can be used in conjunction with prayer and a mantra, simply by placing yourself in this colour before saying the prayer or mantra. Both the colour exercise and a prayer can be used before your start the channelling process.

Symbols

Since time began, symbols have been used as forms of protection. They were, and still are, constructed outwardly, for people to see. Now, as we enter an age of the mind, we are also learning to use them inwardly.

Symbols can affect our mood, making us feel calm or agitated, serene or fearful, happy or sad and so on. This is demonstrated today in the power of advertising, where symbolic images are used to enhance the attractiveness of a product – for example, the strength of a lion depicting a Peugeot car, or an umbrella to show protection as used by Legal and General Insurance and the Abbey National.

Used as a protection, a symbol represents an accepted level of understanding which carries a collective energy that can be very powerful. In Christianity, the cross has become an accepted symbol of spiritual energy that has the power to reject evil. If you are going to use a symbol for personal protection, it is important to use the one that feels right for you.

Paul Diel, author of *Le Symbolisme dans la mythologie grecque* (Symbolism in Greek Mythology) considers the symbol to be 'a precise and crystallised means of expression'. Thus it enables us to focus various concepts of how we need to protect into one symbolised picture or drawing. This is its strength; its weakness lies in its rigidity.

There are three basic symbols:

Most symbols are made up of combinations of these three, and below are some examples for you to meditate on. Each symbol carries a quality of its own, and it is helpful if you can choose one that you feel comfortable with, although they each represent slightly different aspects of protection. They work on subtle levels and you can experiment with them to test how you respond to them.

Centre of infinity; emanation or first cause. Useful for centring or grounding yourself.

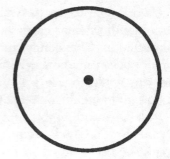

A very powerful symbol. Represents planet Earth and also the four elements of air, fire, earth and water. Very useful for protecting yourself or another. In your mind, place yourself in the centre of the cross and visualise this cross as multidimensional within a golden sphere. You can, in your mind, adjust the size of the cross and sphere so that it can just encompass you, or it can be enlarged to include yourself and others, the room you are working in, the car you are driving in, the house you are living in and so forth. It also has the added benefit of protecting you against malicious thoughts and negative energies as, being a golden sphere, it will merely reflect those unwanted thoughts straight back to their source. Highly recommended.

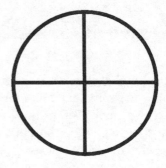

A safe and rigid structure which you can use as an overall protection for you and your family. Seen on most British road signs!

Star of David (or Seal of Solomon). Symbol of the joining of the conscious and unconscious, of Heaven descending and Earth ascending. It is an excellent balancing symbol – the star also stands for the forces of spirit, struggling against the forces of darkness.

The Pentacle, or five-pointed star, reaching up into the higher spheres. As far back as the days of Ancient Egypt it signified 'rising upward towards the point of origin'. (The upper point needs to be vertical.)

Ankh, the symbol of Isis, the Mother God, representing spirit over matter and unconditional love. Very personally protective.

Yin-yang symbol, Chinese in origin. Represents the inflow and outflow of energy, each side containing the seed of its opposite. Masculine/yang and feminine/yin energies. Light and shadow.

The examples I have given offer qualities that will cover most of your needs in the area of psychic protection. But please bear in mind that, whatever way you choose to protect yourself, you need to apply it before every attempt to channel.

Exercise: Protecting your partner

PREPARATION
Sit opposite each other. A is Coverer (protector), B is Receiver. Both should relax well, using the body relaxation techniques described on pp. 34–6. Centre yourselves and attune together. A should visualise you both contained within a bubble of light.

1. Using one of the three protective colours, white, blue or gold, A then visualises and projects it to B, enveloping him/her in the colour. Hold the image for about fifteen seconds, then relax and centre. Repeat with a second colour and, finally, with the third colour.

2. Share your findings. Was there a difference between the three colours? Which colour was easiest to project?

3. Repeat, with B as Coverer and A as Receiver.

4. Share again.

5. A chooses one of the three basic symbols: a circle, an equidistant cross or a triangle, and projects the image, either to surround B or to place it on top of his/her head. Hold for fifteen seconds, then relax and centre. Repeat with a second symbol and, finally, with the third symbol.

6. Share your findings and the different feelings/imagery with each symbol.

7. Repeat with B as Coverer and A as Receiver, and share again.

Issuing a Challenge

What do you do if, whilst relaxing and preparing for channelling, you feel some form of external influence that you are unable to recognise? The answer is: you challenge it. A challenge is, in effect, a means of asking a spirit to identify itself by name, light, colour or symbol. Jesus said, 'Test ye the spirits that they be of the light.' He knew that deception can be a part of life, both in and out of incarnation. He also knew that a challenge evokes an answer. So when I feel *any* energy around me, even H-A, I believe it is my responsibility to challenge it. How is this done?

It is general, when challenging, to invoke the energy of a higher power. This you do by visualising your chosen symbol and then saying: 'In the name of (the Father/Mother God, or whatever deity feels the most powerful to you), show me your light!' When it is a spirit or energy with which I am familiar, I use the equidistant cross in a golden sphere and then the words: 'If you are who you say you are, show me your light!' That is, identify yourself!

Having challenged, you then need to be receptive to any name, light/colour or symbol that comes into your mind or that you inwardly see or feel. It will generally be instantaneous, so do not wait for any length of time. If you get no response or one that is unsatisfactory, issue the challenge three times, in accordance with the Law of Three Requests. This is a powerful universal law and reiterates the challenge to progressively deeper levels. If it is a bona fide spirit, it will not mind being challenged. If it is not, it will go away,

Consider a parallel situation in physical life. If a stranger came to the front door of your house, you would not let him or her in until you were satisfied about their identity. This exercise is performing a similar function and, in the half-century during which I have worked psychically, I have never known my challenge to fail.

Exercise: Challenging your partner

It is important that you practise this exercise before making any attempts at channelling. The idea is to enable both of you to know what it feels like when you challenge and receive an answer to your challenge, and also what it feels like when you are challenged.

PREPARATION
As before, sit opposite each other with A as Coverer/ Protector and B as Receiver. Relax, centre yourselves and attune together.

1. A then visualises a symbol and projects it from his/her mind to B. In this case, you are in effect challenging the essence of the Receiver (B) at a deep level.

2. A will be conscious of making this thought projection and then immediately being receptive to some kind of symbolic response. This may be a light or a colour, a symbol, or a symbolic image or feeling which expresses something of the essential quality of B. Since, in this exercise, the two of you will know each other, it is just possible that for a few seconds A will experience a sense of spiritual oneness with B.

3. During this process, B will remain passive. Despite B's stillness, he/she may sense what A is doing. If the two of you find this or the preceding exercise difficult, remember that the harder you try, the less likely you are to get a result. The way to do it is to try and relax and just allow it to happen. If it doesn't happen the first time, try the exercise again.

4. When the exercise is completed, centre yourselves, make sure that you are both grounded and exchange experiences.

5. Now repeat the exercise the other way round, with B sending to A. Share experiences and see how it worked this time.

6. It is recommended that the exercise should also be practised using one of the other forms of challenge described earlier in this chapter.

Further Preparation for Channelling

It is important to approach channelling with due respect and take one step at a time, gently building the foundations of understanding and technique. In this section I would like to set out some simple basic rules:

Intentions

Psychic energy and other levels of consciousness will always respond to your intentions, so ensure that you know what your intentions are and that they are selfless. If you are using psychic energy to manipulate, you will draw manipulative energies towards you and they will rebound on you in one way or another. So avoid the ego-trap.

Balanced living

A good healthy nutritional diet will help to keep your whole system in balance. Psychic awareness is about working in harmony with the rhythms of the body and nature as a whole.

LIQUIDS

Psychic energy tends to dehydrate you (see p. 86). Coffee and tea are both diuretics and will dehydrate you even more. They are also stimulants and, in some cases, can affect your channelling by making you too tense. Here is a good old naturopathic recommendation: drink two litres of water a day, preferably mineral or filtered, and not with food.

SOLID FOODS

Heavy meats do not encourage the reception of the finer energies, so it is better to avoid them if possible, but it is all right to eat poultry and fish. I must emphasise that this advice is given to enable you to lighten the frequency of your own body and not necessarily for moral reasons. The question of a vegetarian or partly vegetarian diet must relate to personal feelings and choice. Try to eat as nature intended:

- one salad meal a day
- avoid added sugar and salt (if you feel you must use salt, use a brand which is light on sodium chloride and has potassium chloride as its main ingredient. This will be kinder on the blood pressure)
- avoid too many saturated fats
- eat plenty of fruit and vegetables

- only use extra virgin cold-pressed olive oil (it is mono-saturated and one of the safest oils to use)

Last but not least, try some organically grown foods; they are now proven to be more nutritious, taste better and carry a better vibrational energy. Prepare your food with love, then eat it slowly, chewing well in a relaxed way.

Whilst none of these suggestions is essential for doing psychic work, they will help you to be in control, make you healthier and keep you fit. They will also help you to harmonise and resonate with some of the finer energy levels.

ALCOHOL, SMOKING AND HALLUCINOGENIC DRUGS
It is important to avoid alcohol for at least twelve hours before attempting any psychic work, because it temporarily weakens your ability to control your aura. Heavy smoking could also cause problems.

If you are on hard drugs, I would consider any form of psychic work to be highly dangerous because control of your psyche will have been seriously weakened. In this category I include hallucinogenic drugs, especially some of the designer drugs such as ecstasy, and tranquillisers. In fact this warning covers any form of medication that is preventing you from being properly in control of your faculties and loosens the control of the spirit over its own vehicle.

SEX
I am often asked about sex in relation to psychic work, and there are two observations I would like to make. Firstly, it is not a good idea to have sex before channelling as the act briefly depletes you of life force, which may affect the overall balance of your subtle bodies and chakras. Secondly, when you first start experiencing psychic energy it will intensify your whole metabolism and many people find that they become sexually stimulated. This is nothing to worry about, but you need to know how to disperse the feeling. Centre yourself and mentally

spread the energy beyond the sacral/sexual chakra into the whole chakric system, equalising it from base to crown, and ground yourself.

SUPPORT THE NERVOUS SYSTEM

All forms of psychic work can tax the nervous system, so I recommend taking a vitamin B complex supplement. I advise a B complex which is in a food state as it is more fully absorbed into the body. A normal recommended daily dose should be adequate. Buy a good brand – with vitamins, like any other things in life, you get what you pay for!

Don't get a shock!

Many psychic people find that their energy affects or is affected by electrical circuits and that when they are carrying out psychic work electric light bulbs often blow, fuses will burn out and so on. I used to think that I was not personally affected by this lack of resonance with electrical frequencies, but recently I have found it difficult to wear my quartz watch when channelling or healing. I find myself becoming very conscious of it and the frequency that it seems to emanate feels discordant with my own psychic frequencies; so I take it off on these occasions.

So don't be worried if this kind of reaction occurs for you. At least you will know that your inflow or outflow of psychic energy is working.

Patience

Remember the old adage: 'When the pupil is ready, the door opens.' Things happen for us when we deal with any blockages in our lives and create space for movement forward.

Be in control

Make sure that you are centred and grounded before you start any form of psychic work. Always be in control. Prepare yourself by means of a short 'quiet time', attunement or meditation. Don't work unless you feel that it is OK for you to do so. Also check that you are centred and grounded when you have finished the psychic work you have been doing.

Ask for help

Don't forget that if you have a problem that you don't understand, it's all right to seek advice.

A Recommended Daily Routine

As a working psychic, channeller and healer, as well as offering counselling and nutritional advice I need to have a daily routine in order to keep myself in balance, harmonised and free of any unwanted negative energies. Here are details of this routine in the hope that you will find it helpful.

First part

CLEANSING MYSELF
Sometimes you may feel 'tacky', in the sense of being aware of uncomfortable energies around you. I would like to share a simple technique which I have recommended to many clients and students and which I find extremely effective.

Exercise: Sieving

1. Sit down, lie down or stand up. Visualise a garden sieve in your hands. It will be circular, with a mesh that can sieve out whatever your mind determines.

2. Start at your feet and bring the sieve up through your subtle bodies, chakras, physical body and aura, sieving out,

81

in your mind, any unwanted thoughts. Bring the sieve above your head. As you do so, close an imaginary trapdoor just above your head so that the contents of the sieve cannot re-enter your being.

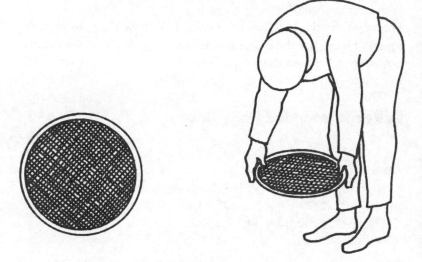

3. After closing the trapdoor, empty the contents of the sieve into a bag, seal it and send it off to its rightful place in the universe, wherever that may be.

4. Repeat the exercise three times, each time using a sieve with a finer mesh. The last time, the sieve's mesh will be so fine that it will be like a coffee filter.

Second part

BALANCING MYSELF

Here, I use the balancing exercise involving the overhead projector given in Chapter 5 (p. 41). This time, it is helpful to be aware of the correlation between the seven colours of the spectrum used in the exercise and the different energies of the seven major chakras. However, it is not necessary actively to visualise the individual chakras when dong the exercise.

Third part

PROTECTING MYSELF

Having cleared and balanced myself, I am now ready to protect myself. Here I use the multi-dimensional equidistant cross within a golden sphere, as described on p. 72. Any therapist will find this three-part exercise particularly helpful.

Finally, I would like to repeat that I consider it essential to use psychic protection techniques if you are going to practise channelling.

CHAPTER 9

How to Start Channelling

'We can optimise that which we are; we can optimise that which we have; we can optimise that which we create.'

H-A

In the preceding chapters I have given a broad understanding of what channelling is and what it offers, leading on to learning how to identify energies and be in control of the subtler aspects of your being. We have looked at the various ways in which we can safeguard ourselves, using different forms of psychic protection. It is important that you should have carried out the various exercises in preparation for actual channelling. In this chapter I shall help you to work through the channelling process, step-by-step.

Preparation

Choose a favourite space, a room where you and your partner in this work will feel really comfortable and relaxed and can spend an hour without being interrupted. Remember to unplug the telephone and to make sure that there are no pet animals in the room, as both cats and dogs are very psychic animals and can react quite strongly when they become aware of increased psychic energy.

Many years ago, when I was channelling in someone else's house, I remember asking my hostess to put her cat outside the room while the channelling was in progress. She waited until I had started and then decided to let the cat back into the room, no doubt thinking that I was being over-particular and that it would not matter. Once back inside, the cat felt the increased psychic energy, came straight across the room, jumped on to my lap and, in its most friendly way, dug its claws into my thighs – in fairness, probably to get into a more comfortable position! In those days I used to go into quite a deep form of trance, and in this state it was easy for my spirit to leave my body – a practice which is unnecessary for channelling. In this situation I was very vulnerable, and the sudden shock of the cat's claws entering my flesh brought my spirit back into my body with a most unpleasant jolt. It was a very painful and potentially dangerous experience.

I can vividly remember finding myself coming straight out of the trance state and lying on the floor in a foetal position, feeling as if someone wearing army boots had kicked me in the solar plexus. I was in agony until I could rebalance my aura and my chakras. Fortunately, there was someone in the room who was looking after me psychically and was able to help me rebalance myself. So beware – don't think that *your* dog or cat will behave itself perfectly!

Setting the Scene

I find it is really worth taking the trouble to set the scene: have some fresh flowers or a pot plant in the room, some sympathetic lighting, and maybe burn an aromatic oil. (Vetivert is a good one if you find it difficult to ground yourself.) A lighted candle is always a good point of focus in the room. Prepare the space psychically by standing in the middle of the room, placing yourself and your partner in the centre of an equidistant cross within the golden sphere and then allowing that symbol to expand until it encompasses the entire room. In the expansion of the symbol, you are literally sweeping any negative or unpleasant energies out of the room. Have a plentiful supply of mineral or filtered water available and drink a couple of glasses before you start. There are two reasons for this: firstly, psychic energy tends to dehydrate you, and secondly, water acts as an excellent conductor of psychic energy, enhancing your psychic state of awareness. I know a number of psychics who get flashes of inspiration whilst going to the loo!

It is also advisable not to have a heavy meal beforehand. It can not only make you feel sleepy, but also create a heaviness that will certainly make it more difficult to become sensitively aware. Make sure you have a pad and pencil and/or a tape recorder to record your experiences.

Is there a special way to sit? If you know yoga I would suggest the lotus position (see p. 35); but only if you can be completely comfortable and relaxed in this position and are able to sustain it for a period of time.

Otherwise, and for most Western people, I recommend the Egyptian position (see p. 35): sit on an upright chair keeping your back straight, your hands on your knees with the palms of your hands facing upwards for receptivity – just like one of those Egyptian statues. Do not cross your legs or hands; if you do, you will effectively cut off your receptivity to inflowing energy. (As a matter of interest, crossing your arms and legs is one way of protecting yourself, which is why the arms of a dead person are crossed – an old ritual to give the person protection on the next stage of their journey.)

It is a good idea to agree with your partner a time limit for the whole exercise; if not, you can become exhausted if you carry on for too long. Twenty to thirty minutes would seem reasonable in the beginning.

Attunement

Spend a few minutes attuning within and harmonising with you partner, maybe focusing on the candle flame. This is the moment for you both to build a protective bubble around the two of you, using a symbol you have agreed upon. Now you will be ready to start a relaxation exercise, so as to become aware.

Relaxation

One way to relax the body is to do the exercise described on pp. 35–6, where you start with your toes, feel them, tense them and then relax them, moving up the body in this fashion until you have allowed each part to relax in sequence. Another method is as follows:

1. Breathe deeply and comfortably.

2. On the in-breath, feel that you are drawing in energy from the cosmos and that it is travelling right down your body into your pelvic area.

3. On the out-breath, feel that you are exhaling any tensions, whether emotional or physical. Breathe out all the fear, stresses and strains of your life, naming them mentally and releasing them. Repeat this breath as necessary.

4. On the next deep breath, feel that you are breathing the energy in as before and then on the out-breath send it right down your legs through your knees, calves, ankles and feet to your toes, filling every cell with energy.

5. Carry on, breathing this cosmic energy into your shoulders, down your arms and into your hands and fingers.

6. Then do the same up through the neck, throat, facial muscles, eyes and scalp.

7. You will now feel both energised and relaxed, and aware of yourself as a whole being. Sense the integration of your various levels of consciousness: the subtle bodies, the chakras and the aura.

8. Mentally reconnect with your partner, sending him/her a thought of wellbeing and unconditional love, thus bringing the atmosphere in the room into a state of harmony and readiness to start the process of becoming aware.

Becoming Aware

From now on, the coverer is the one who must remain psychically grounded and responsible for sustaining protection around the channeller. This protection needs to be spherical, using white, blue or gold, and of a fine filigree nature so that only the finer, more spiritual frequencies may reach the channeller (see the exercises in Chapter 8). Give the protection a mental top-up from time to time during the session, projecting a challenge if a presence is felt.

The next step is for you, the channeller, to relax your mind completely and become aware of the atmosphere around your head and shoulders. Gently send out a 'radar' signal in your mind that revolves 360 degrees around you, so as to pick up any other level of consciousness that may lie outside your normal level of experience. Keep in touch with your coverer verbally at intervals, or when he/she asks what you are feeling or sensing. It is important that you both keep in touch with what you, the channeller, are experiencing, even though you may be in a slightly altered state of consciousness.

The important consideration when you are trying to receive is to keep your mind completely open and avoid any form of expectation. Do not try to analyse or interpret what you experience at this stage.

What are you likely to find when you begin to place yourself in this state of awareness? There are many possibilities. You could experience colour, music, inspiration, symbols or shapes. You may hear a voice or receive a word or a sentence. Or you may become aware of a presence somewhere around you, to the side or behind, or even overshadowing you. The presence could be your own personal guide or some other form of external guidance.

Challenge

This is the moment for both of you to challenge the presence. If you do not like the 'feel' of it, make the challenge stronger. Do it three times, if necessary. Should you still feel uncomfortable, close the energy down, re-centre yourselves and terminate the session. This is an unlikely eventuality, but it could connect with your own energy being disturbed or fearful for some reason. It could also reflect the atmosphere in the room, which you may need to cleanse and prepare more thoroughly. Remember, you are moving into very subtle and sensitive levels of awareness and the atmosphere in which you work plays an important role. Accept the situation as part of the learning process and remedy what you feel is the problem next time. Seek help if necessary.

Let's return to our session, assuming that all is well and the response to your challenge feels good.

The Channelling Session

You, the channeller, may find at first that you simply get the feeling that you have made a 'connection'. You have *felt* a presence, *received* a thought, *seen* a colour. That's fine. Positive and good. You may have some words you wish to relay, 'I am being told . . .' That's fine. Positive and good. Give yourself permission to speak your impressions, however faint they may be. If a presence is strong, you may even feel the urge to relay a message more directly, as from the presence itself: 'Good evening. I have something I wish to say' or 'I have a message for the channeller herself/himself.'

The coverer needs to respond encouragingly: questioning as in ordinary conversation will help the flow to continue. Here are some examples of the type of questions I would ask:

- 'Greetings, may we ask you to tell us something about yourself?'
- 'Are you young or old?'
- 'Are you male or female?'
- 'When were you last incarnate, and was it on this planet?'
- 'What did you do and where did you live in your last life?
- 'When were you born and when did you die?'
- 'Are you the personal guide of the channel?'
- If not, 'Are you a guide who has come to help him/her with a specific problem?'
- 'What is the area of your help?'
- 'Have you ever communicated through a channel or sensitive before?'
- 'If so, whom?'

And of course, one can go on. What is important is to encourage the communication and flow of energy through the channeller, which strengthens the link between the spirit entity and the mind of the channel.

In addition to my questions, I would also be putting out a thought to settle and stabilise the atmosphere in the room.

'H-A, can you tell us about the relationship between the sensitive and yourself?'

'The energy created between the sensitive and myself is a kind of bond that exists and which can exist for every person incarnate on this planet at this time. I have heard much talk about the use of the word "channelling" and I would like to progress it a little further so that you can see it, not just as a means for you as a person in a physical body to be in touch with other levels of consciousness, but much more as a kind of bonding between your outer consciousness and your inner consciousness. And it is through that bonding that you can access these more subtle levels of understanding.

If humanity is going to emerge through the next hundred years with a great deal more wisdom and understanding than it has at present, the understanding of that bonding is essential; for, it is only through such bonding that the higher and wiser aspects of being can manifest.'

H-A

Closing the Scene

When you feel the psychic energy waning, or you have been channelling for about twenty minutes, both of you need to close down and ground yourselves. First of all, spare a thought of thanks to those unseen helpers who have been there for you and have protected and helped you during the session. Then gently allow the energy to subside and become aware of your physical bodies once again. This time, do it in reverse order to that used when you were preparing to channel.

Feel the atmosphere around your head gradually settling down, and allow your conscious mind to resume control. Become aware of your head and scalp, facial muscles, tongue, jaw, throat, neck, shoulders, arms, hands and fingers, spine, pelvic area, thighs, knees, ankles, feet and toes. Really *think* the energy down, right down through your feet, extending roots into the ground. If necessary, use some of the grounding procedures outlined in Chapter 5.

At the end of a session it is always a good idea to follow the recommended daily routine of sieving, centring yourself, balancing the aura and visualising the symbol of protection (see p. 81). It clears the mind, focuses the brain, brings you down to earth and protects you.

This is the time to note what took place, providing a valuable record of how you are progressing. Include the date, time, location and names of any friends present, together with anything unusual that happened. Lastly, plug in the telephone again and have a cup of tea!

Practising channelling needs to be done on a regular basis but not too often, as you need to become gently and rhythmically in tune with the psychic energies you are contacting. A weekly session would be ideal, although some people may find twice a week acceptable. See what suits you, If you find yourself fatigued, over-tense or disorientated in any way, either you are doing it too often and need to lengthen the time between each practice, or you are not grounding yourself properly after the sessions.

It is difficult to be precise about how long it will take before you get a tangible result. Interestingly, I have found that those who develop slowly and gradually are those who find it the most satisfactory and fulfilling in the long term. So if it doesn't all ⤺ happen at once, don't despair − keep going, keep relaxed and allow it to happen gradually in a gentle, unhurried way.

CHAPTER 10

What Are
the Effects
of Channelling?

*'Channelling is primarily a means for individuals to broaden
their level of awareness, so that they can discover the karma of this
particular incarnation.'*

H-A

On a psychic level, channelling involves allowing energies to flow
through us which are of a finer frequency or vibration than that
which comprises our physical and various subtle bodies. These
energies interconnect with all different levels of our being, so
that the physical, emotional, mental and spiritual levels are all
involved. Once we have decided to activate that channelling
process, we have pointed ourselves to change. One thing is for
sure – life will never be the same once you have started to channel! It offers incredible benefits, but also sets deep and sometimes
difficult challenges. Let's look at some of the benefits and some
of the challenges:

The Benefits of Channelling

- It will lead to an expanded level of consciousness and
  understanding, including heightened levels of perception
- It will occasionally enable us to find what Joseph Campbell,
  one of the greatest authorities on mythology in modern

93

times, described as states of bliss, finding peace and inner harmony

- You will uncover the awareness that truth lies in the eye of the beholder and that there are no *absolute truths* (see diagram below). To find absolute truth is to grow beyond the need of it
- You will be able to find self-empowerment and self-realisation
- Your own altered states of consciousness and understanding will enable others to grow and find their way forward in this life
- You will be able to perceive and understand other worlds and psychic realms

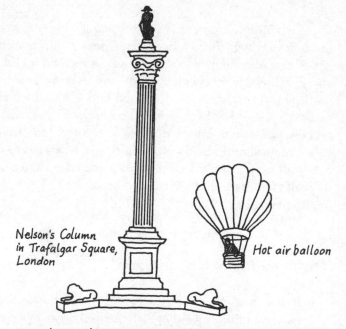

Column of Truth

Nelson's Column
in Trafalgar Square,
London

Hot air balloon

As the balloon rises, we see Truth
in a wider perspective and understanding

Let's imagine that we are in a hot air balloon taking off from Trafalgar Square in London. If the balloon rises fifteen feet we see the paving stones. This, at the moment, is our truth.

As our life and evolution grow, so the balloon soars higher. As it reaches fifty feet, we again look over the side of the basket. This time we see the whole of Trafalgar Square – pigeons, people, buses, taxis, cars, buildings and so on. It is the same truth, but from a wider perspective of understanding. When the balloon reaches the top of Nelson's column and we look over the side of the basket, we see now the whole of greater London in which there are 12 million people living, dying, experiencing. This is our *ultimate truth* on this particular journey.

The Challenges of Channelling

- Channelling tends to act as a light shining in the darkness, revealing our inner blockages, the negative aspects of our personality that bring to the surface our repressed feelings and conflicts. This can create wide mood swings as we find ourselves facing our shadow. It can create a period of intense self-examination, maybe with a counsellor or psychotherapist on issues such as an unsatisfactory job or relationship, which could precipitate action.

- It enables us to accept that we are all different and that words such as 'better' or 'worse', 'right' or 'wrong', take on different meanings. All these challenges emphasise that in the practice of channelling it is essential to work within as a discipline and constantly to align, refocus and balance our subtle bodies, aura and chakras.

- States of slight mental disassociation and feeling unfocused can cause headaches and possible nausea. These states can happen through faulty psychic procedures and through intensive or insensitive experimentation. It is important to follow all the steps described in this book.

- Psychologically, we can face an identity crisis (who am I?), especially if we find our friends and those around us relating to the guidance that is being channelled through us. This can feel quite disempowering.

- In the same vein, it can also create the problem of dealing with those who seek to put *you* on a pedestal because of the wisdom or advice that is coming from the guide.

It is important, therefore, that we keep clear boundaries between who we feel we are and owning our own part in the procedure; and all the other levels of communication that will be going on around us.

Creativity and Intention

'H-A, I would like to ask about creativity. When ideas start to flow how does one know whether these ideas are being inspired by one's soul, one's Higher Self or one's guiding spirit? And what is creative genius?'

'When people start to honour their own sense of awareness, this is a moment when they are ready to allow the flow of creativity through them. Channelling, as I see it and as I have talked about it through the sensitive, concerns that concept. Every spirit within a human body has a Higher Self, and when one starts to find that stillness within and allow a deeper, more receptive state of consciousness to come forward into your mind, that is when the creativity starts. And this is how I would like to see people grow and extend their understanding. In one sense, from my perspective it is irrelevant whether it is their own Higher Self that is inspiring them, their personal

96

guide/guardian angel, or whether it is from a source that extends beyond to some other level of consciousness.

'Now if the level of consciousness lies beyond the person, she/he will very likely at first be contacting a level of being of a departed soul. Let me digress a little here.

'When you die your spirit leaves your body and finds itself in a kind of resting place which is a plane of existence very close in vibration to planet Earth. At first it may feel confused and, in some cases, very earthbound depending on the type of "death" it has experienced, sudden or otherwise, and also the state of mind in which it passed over. Eventually, this changes as the spirit has a greater realisation of what has happened to it. In other words, with the help of other spirits, it wakes up to its new reality. It then moves forward into a state of being in which it is able to look back over the life it has led, compare it with its overall karma – its experience in all its lives so far – and consider why it chose that particular body and whether it has fulfilled its purpose in that lifetime. It will take some time to come to terms with all that has happened in that life.

'It is rather similar to situations when you are actually incarnate in the physical body, understanding that your past is a history that has formulated your present being. It is very easy to get caught up in that past and to find certain parts of it unacceptable and difficult to face, areas that your psychologists would call "unresolved issues".

'If the spirit is unable to come to terms with unresolved issues on that plane of rest, it will of course carry them forward into its next life; and it will want to use that next life to face those very issues. Indeed, you chose your parents, not primarily for what they are or were, but for the challenges *you* needed to help you forward in your evolution. Spiritual evolution is about the growth of your capability of understanding.

'So in starting to channel you may at first contact a spirit of a departed soul. With practice you will be able to take your consciousness right beyond that into what would be looked upon as the higher realms, the spiritual realms, levels of thought which move beyond conditional thought and action. In the old days, it would have been most important that those spiritual realms of consciousness that a medium contacted were personified in the name of a departed spirit. This often turned out to be a spirit from a root-race, such as one of the wise ones from the Native American culture.

'What is of importance in channelling is that the person contacts a higher level of creative thought. This enables more advanced teachings and philosophies to be offered to the planet because the evolution of a planet, both individually and collectively, is on-going.

'Let us now look at channelling at the level of genius. In this whole process of evolution some spirits will eventually move on to quite fine levels of consciousness, beyond the need to incarnate physically any more, but they may choose to come back for a specific purpose to bring some quality, maybe of music or art or scientific discovery, to help move the planet forward in its overall evolution. The Godhead does not compel evolution but it likes to be able to stimulate creativity that enables this forward movement in consciousness.

'So a spirit may come back into an Earth body, bringing with it a great deal of wisdom and consciousness that it then has to contain within the limitations of a physical being. This it will find very difficult because of the restrictions of the physical mind and body. Let us say for example the spirit decides to enter the body of a child who will become a composer. Very quickly from a young age, some of this brilliant music will start to come forward. But because the physical body has not been trained to handle its psychic energy, its need for protection, and its need for balance and discipline, the amount of energy that the spirit is producing and pouring through, very often, a frail body can result in a very unbalanced form of living. This is what frequently happens in cases of what you would describe as "genius". And if you look at the history of humankind, many geniuses have had difficult lives for that very reason. I would like to pick one example of a person who had a very difficult life with their creative genius. It is a controversial example but one I think that is very valuable. I would like to speak about the man, Jesus.

'When the Christ consciousness merged with Jesus the man, this was indeed an incredible challenge and is why Jesus the man spent many years in preparation in what the Bible calls the "wilderness". In my understanding, many of these were years spent with the Essenes. The Essenes knew about this incarnation and that it was their task to prepare and train this man to receive this high level of spiritual consciousness. But Jesus the man was a man, Jesus the man was not God. So, the Christ consciousness that streamed into him had to be filtered down, otherwise that high level of energy could have destroyed him.

'The same process of course has applied to other avatars [spiritual masters] who have come to this planet to help move it forward by offering a new concept of behaviour and thinking for their time and their place. And when I talk in this way you can see how important it is that people are flexible in their thinking and are not frightened of letting go of the past.

'This is a very long answer to a very simple question but it is one where I have tried to illustrate how the channelling process works on different levels. I have tried to show that it is a creative communication that can happen on many levels. It can come from or through your Higher Self or your personal guide; it can come from a departed soul or from a spirit from the finer, spiritual realms. It can also come through a creative genius where that soul has the capability of contacting very fine levels of consciousness. But whatever source is contacted, the channeller has the responsibility of handling his or her own energy and merging with that other energy . . .'

'Presuming that the faculty for channelling does not happen automatically, are there forms of work or

**practice one could pursue which would exercise and
start opening up one's ability for channelling? For
example, work like regular writing? I mean
straightforward writing which could become
creative writing. I have been told that guides and
spiritual helpers are always ready and happy to help
in this process. I could also add any other activities
like painting and composing, but writing is the one
that is more direct . . .'**

'Can you please tell me how you see the difference between
"writing" and "creative" writing?'

**'Well, ahhhh. Well, the immediate thing I thought of
is that maybe all writing is creative writing, whether
it is a business report or . . . except I think perhaps a
business report would be more factual writing. I am
getting wound up here . . . [*laughter*].'**

'I seek not to trip you.'

**'I know you don't, I am tripping myself, you don't
have to [*laughter*]. I was really thinking in terms of
any kind of creative work, but particularly writing
because that is the thing that interests me most and
the thing I seem to be doing least. Is the actual act of
writing something which can help to start opening a
channelling facility? To connect one for example
with . . . some other dimension?'**

'Meditation is one way of developing the channelling facility.'

'Yes.'

'Another way certainly is doing an activity that is creative in
itself, and there are a wide range of those, my son, from
writing to painting to gardening to making pottery. So any
activity, if it is approached in an open way, can lead to that
inspirational element being introduced. The important thing

about it is that you allow it to happen naturally. The obstacle that faces most people when they are seeking to stimulate their creativity is that they expect a miracle. Expecting a miracle will always effectively close down your creativity. Similarly, when a person approaches any job or activity with anger, lack of confidence, boredom or feeling disheartened, that draws the curtains on creativity.

'So it is about working regularly in a disciplined way, maybe with a friend, maybe on your own; and noticing how, over a period of time, the activity develops. With most people that activity will develop in a way that will enable them to be in touch with their intuition. It needs to be approached in an open, loving and enjoyable way. Does that answer your question?'

'Yes, but there is still something I am not quite sure about. In the pursuit of any kind of creativity, whether gardening, cooking, or writing . . . can this actually in a sense become a channelling process?'

'Yes.'

'In other words it is almost a synonymous thing. That is really what I was asking. So in pursuing whatever it is, one can actually open up one's channelling capabilities?'

'Absolutely, my son. When you design things with your computer is there not an aspect of that that you find creative?'

'Well, indeed, yes.'

'And satisfying? Because it is stimulating that creative side of you. You see, what I am trying to explain is this. I think it is vitally important for every person to have an activity that stimulates their creativity because in that stimulation lies fulfilment. And when a person is fulfilled they do not need to be aggressive or violent or go to war because they are finding an inner peace. Let me leave you with that answer to think about.' . . .

'Would you say that we are very much closer than we realise to other levels of consciousness, and that there is much more blending and picking up from other levels than . . .'

'Yes, yes, yes, yes! [*with great enthusiasm*]. The whole substance of my teaching on one level is that these areas of spiritual consciousness are available to everybody and they aren't "out there". They are here, just beyond you, and the more you can integrate them into your being, the more fulfilled and awakened you can become. Is that enough?'

'Well, just to say that, acknowledging that there are forces and beings around us that are helping us in one way or another would, I imagine, already open a much better possibility for us to receive help.'

'Around us there is a universe of energy; and in that universe of energy there are billions and billions and billions of spirits seeking, going forward, evolving, seeing the light, dealing with the shadow. Now the great gift that each one of those beings has is that of free will to choose. When you enter a physical body and start your life's journey, you actually have a choice of whether you seek the light or you seek the shadow. So when you talk of all those beings surrounding a person, the type of energies that you attract and that make contact with you depend upon your motivation and intention. If you are seeking personal power, if you want to gain power over others and so hurt others and yourself, if you want to blind yourself to God's universe, then there are energies there that can satisfy that need.

'So, it would be erroneous to suggest that all around you is light; for, as above, so below, and as below, so above. But I cannot say strongly enough that, if your intentions are ultimately to seek and give unconditional love and that you approach this in a disciplined and knowledgeable way, you will find that beauty, that resonance, within and without. And you will move forward in your evolution with greater understanding and compassion . . .'

H-A

Channellers' Experiences

Following, are a few examples of people's experience to illustrate how channelling can unlock blockages and start creativity flowing in a way that enhances life.

The first is a comment from Niels who is Managing Director of a company that develops economic and industrial strategies for governments. He says, 'I participated in the Channelling course during the same year as I completed my healing education at the College of Healing. I also left my employment of ten years and started my own international consultancy company.

'In all these aspects of my life, the channelling training has facilitated an opening up to my inner knowing, my intuition and to my ability to truly understand how other people perceive things. It enables me to make decisions in a much simpler way than before.

'But, most of all, channelling has helped me to "feel" the flow of life and to go with it. It has been the most valuable step in my spiritual development and unfoldment.'

Another concerns Alison who came on the School of Channelling course earlier this year. When she arrived for part 3, I could see she was quite excited. After dinner on the first evening, the group met to share their experiences since taking part 2. When it came to her turn, Alison announced excitedly to the group, 'I've discovered that I can paint!' She then produced some examples of her work which were quite impressive, especially for an untrained first attempt. This discovery had brought a whole new dimension of experience into her life.

Then there is the case of Peter, who is a business consultant. He says, 'Learning to channel has given me my own personal source of knowledge, insight and guidance that I know I can trust. It has quickened the pace of change and made my life and business easier. I feel much more integrated as a person.'

I have also worked with a number of writers who have developed writers' block. This can happen when they have written a number of books, plays, etc and then suffer an emotional trauma such as the loss of a partner. It is as though the shock impedes the creative flow and they find they can no longer access new ideas. Training to channel can re-open those closed doors and release the dam, allowing creativity to flow again. In some cases, it may even flow in a different direction, i.e. a writer may begin to paint, or an artist begin to write poetry.

Finally, here is a summary of the effects felt by channellers:
- loss of balance
- self-doubt
- dealing with people who think you are nuts!
- feeling out of control
- not knowing
- physical problems
- possible partner problems
- loneliness
- fear of delusion
- increased sensitivity
- feeling of exhilaration
- heightened awareness
- love and inner stillness
- confidence and peace

CHAPTER 11

Connecting with
Other Levels
of Consciousness

'A person who is truly humble is a person who has faced their
vulnerability.'

H-A

In an altered state of consciousness such as you will find yourself
in with my gentle but structured approach to channelling, you
first of all access parts of the unconscious that is normally
unavailable to us. This may bring forward comments or answers
that deep down we probably know or understand, but are unable
to access in normal consciousness. This in itself can bring valuable intuitive thoughts to bear on some of the problems we
encounter in everyday life, and help us to utilise our mind more
fully and effectively.

It is through our unconscious that the finer aspect of ourselves, the Higher Self, often speaks to us, maybe through
dreams, sometimes in moments of realisation and inner 'knowing'. And it is our intuitive faculty which links those thoughts to
consciousness. In channelling, therefore, we may well receive
information and inspiration from our own Higher Self; and that
can be a perfectly valid form of channelling

We can also reach out, beyond the limitation of our own
being, to other more subtle and wiser levels of consciousness that
are in a position to have a wider overview because they are not in
an incarnate state. One important being who may well wish to

105

communicate through us and to us is our own personal guide; when working in this way we need to make a good connection with it, as it will support us and help us in this work.

Our Personal Guide

Each one of us has a personal guide, sometimes called a guardian angel, which is usually a spirit that has experienced being in a physical human body and wishes to give support to another spirit that is incarnate, such as you or me. This personal guide joins us at the moment of conception and leaves at the moment of death. It is not there to live our life for us; it is there to give support and help look after us during our waking life, and perhaps even more so when we are asleep. This is a time when the spirit can and does wander from the body, exploring the planes of existence. In this state, known as 'astral travel', we would be extremely vulnerable without some form of external protection as provided by our personal guide. Some people develop the ability to 'astrally travel' when fully conscious, but this lies outside the naturally provided protection of the personal guide and can be a dangerous practice. I would not recommend it.

If leaving the body in this way 'just happens,' you need to practise the grounding exercises so that you can gain greater control over the subtler levels of your being.

'You say that we each have a guardian angel that remains with us to help and protect us during this lifetime. As I am starting to learn to channel, would it be helpful to make a connection with my guardian angel, and if so, how would I do that?'

'Your guardian angel is with you from the moment you join the physical body at conception to the moment it leaves the body at death. A guardian angel is there as a support; it is there to help you when you need that help. It is also there to

106

protect you when you are in sleep state, when your body recharges itself rather like a battery being recharged. Because in that state you are vulnerable in that your spirit leaves your body, also to be recharged. And so your guardian angel is there to protect you. My advice to anyone who wishes to start channelling, is that it can be to your advantage to become aware of your guardian angel or, as I would prefer to call it, your "personal guide".

'The way to contact your personal guide is simply to ask for it to make itself known. Most personal guides can operate much more efficiently and lovingly if there is a closer liaison between them and the spirit of the person concerned. So if a partnership can be established between the two of you, then the results will be very much more fruitful. And if you reach a state in which you want to channel beyond your personal guide to some other level of consciousness, it will be there to support you in that need.

'Having said that, I would like to add that a total awareness of your personal guide is *not* necessary in order to channel. It is an aid and it is a very nice thing to happen for both the person and for the personal guide; but it is not essential in the channelling process. It is not essential in that aspect of the channelling process in which you become aware beyond yourself of another level of consciousness.'

H-A

'Thank you.'

If the personal approach is the one that works for you and you start to become aware of your personal guide, try and find out more about it. Does it feel as though it is male or female? Young or old? What part of the world does it associate itself with? Does it have a name. If so, what is it? Agree a symbol or some way in which you can always recognise it. Really get to know it, but do *not* expect it to be God!

Where Will Channelling Take You?

I sometimes meet people who say, after attempting to channel, 'Well, it was interesting, but I'm not sure where it is leading me.' Then six months or a year later, they will get in touch and say, 'It's quite extraordinary, but all sorts of things have started to happen in my life.'

This is the area where this 'loosening up' of the psyche can also help to bring forward dormant emotional problems and lead people into finding solutions to their difficulties. We can so easily feel trapped and unable to move forward in our lives, and clearer intuitive contact with our Higher Self and/or our personal guide can be extremely helpful in clarifying and guiding us through what may feel like rocky waters. I often wonder how many people in psychotherapy and counselling could really enhance the process by training to channel. In my experience, the number would be very high.

In 'becoming aware' there are no fixed rules – it is how it is for you, and you are unique. So it will always be useful to compare what happens for you with other people's experiences, for they will give you further ideas and perspectives.

Initiation – Lifting Your Spirit into a New Focus

'This evening I would like to encapsulate my thoughts on "initiation", a word much used in the past; perhaps a word to be avoided at the present time. But it depends on how you see and understand that word. I cannot emphasise strongly enough that life in the physical body is about a series of initiations – initiations that are based on the understanding and the wisdom of your own individual Higher Self.

'One major challenge that faces human life in the physical body is that of "time", for time brings "impatience": "I have got to reach that corner by such and such a time"; "I have to reach that standard, otherwise I will fail." But life need not be about failure. Equally, life need not be about success. In actuality, life is about "experience"; and the more you can allow your inner Being to come through, to flow and to move with universal energies, the less painful these initiations are. They become painful because we *expect*. They become painful because we *demand*, and we demand because we are *needy*.

'Every day in your life is like the sun rising in the morning, bringing with it new hope, new light, new vision to nourish your needs; and this helps you forward, to make you understand that there are universal rhythms that lie beyond the rhythms of physical life. It is not easy to talk about these universal rhythms because they are like frequencies that resonate, and that resonance can lift your spirit into a new focus, into a new level of understanding.

'That is what I understand by *initiation*. It is nothing to do with reaching that corner by that time, or *else*; or with suffering for the sake of suffering. Your whole culture has been built up on such concepts.

'As we move into the new consciousness of the Aquarian Age, a whole new set of values are presenting themselves – values that relate to your own inner being and the way in which you allow your life to unfold. This means looking and reflecting on your life and understanding, that it has moved at a pace which is OK; and that you can *accept* that that is the pace at which it has moved and that it is OK. Immediately you introduce, "Why did I do that? Why am I stuck here? Why didn't I do that before? Why did I meet this person in the first place? What do I expect from them?" and, even worse, "What do I expect from me?" you sabotage yourself. And these are the saboteurs that I am privileged to lead you beyond, because in my world they don't exist.

'My world is made up of universal rhythms – rhythms that you can either resist with that type of rigid expectation and non-acceptance, or rhythms that you can step into and allow yourself to go forward, unfolding, rejoicing, understanding that everything that is and has been has meaning and validity. Understanding that whatever you find difficult in your life, right now, is an important challenge for you. Allow these challenges, these initiations, to happen for you. Stop trying to manipulate them; that is not control, that is stupidity. Handling your life is about acknowledging and understanding. It is about being aware and allowing; and being aware and allowing means that you are stripping your whole life of rigidity. You are making a statement saying, "I am no longer afraid, I do not need fear, for fear engulfs me, fear prevents me, fear sabotages me."

'On one level I am setting standards that you may regard as impracticable and impossible to achieve. Everything is possible, but this is about allowing yourself to take that quantum leap. It is not a leap into the darkness; it is not even a leap into the beyond. *It is a leap out of your stuckness.*

'You have each chosen this life because it is presenting you with the opportunities, the challenges, to do just that. You won't fail. There is no such thing as failure anyway. It is all in the mind. *Freedom is a state of mind, not a state of being.* You can have that freedom, you can exercise it, use it, tell others about it. The only miracles that exist, dear friends, are those that you create. For no spirit of wisdom is going to collude with creating miracles unless you are ready to make them or receive them.

'If you stand up and say, "I am not going to do this any more. I am going to step out of my stuckness, be my own person and lead my life in my own way, with unconditional love and accepting support from my fellow beings", then it will happen. For you will tune into those universal rhythms, that divine energy that will uplift your spirit and take you beyond need, beyond greed, with the opportunity of growing the seed of the next step on your evolutionary path.

'You need to stand up and be counted because you came into this life with a very definite mission. Each and every one of you has a spiritual mission, and let us be very clear about what I mean by a spiritual mission. I don't mean that you have to go and squat at the top of a mountain [*laughter*], two mountains actually [*more laughter*], because my mountains are about acknowledging the joy and wonder of experiencing in a physical body. Spirituality is about completeness, wholeness and forgiveness. It is not about being "right" and knowing all the answers, for there are no answers. It is about acknowledging that warmth within and saying . . .

'"I am ready to step forward! I know I am part of a corporate energy that is here on this planet, enabling it to go forward from one age into the next. I have chosen this life to be part of that corporate energy. I now have choice. I can either allow myself to become part of that energy or I can paddle my own canoe."

'There is no right answer to that and you do not earn brownie points by making what you consider to be a "right" decision, for whatever decision you make, it will add to your wisdom and understanding.

'But if you want to take the "high road", which means taking the reins of the challenges that you meet, I can promise you riches of experience, riches of understanding, riches of beingness and of being able to see what a wondrous opportunity life in the physical body really is. Take it with both hands! Hold it up and allow it to lead you forward into the greater wisdom of the universe.

'Have faith. Have faith in yourself, in what you are here for. Have love, love for yourself and all those around you. Let go of your inner saboteur and strive forward in confidence, knowing that there is beauty, wisdom and understanding around each corner. Be part of those universal rhythms.'

H-A

CHAPTER 12

It's Important
to Have Doubts

'The moment of finding your importance is the moment of losing it.'
H-A

There cannot be a channeller who does not have doubts about his/her channelling. If they claim not to have any doubts, that is the time to start questioning the results. The questions that arise most often are:

- 'Am I really doing it?'
- 'Is it just my imagination?'
- 'Is there a guide or some form of guidance present?'
- 'Why me?'

On one hand it is important to be discriminating; on the other, you have to trust in the process.

The Saboteur

It is helpful to understand why these doubts are necessary, and this correlates to our evolutionary growth in the sense that, as the positive side of you grows, so does the more negative side. This growth challenges our status quo. All change can be scary, and suddenly to find out that a whole new side of your personality is beginning to emerge is highly challenging – particularly as this can be a side of you which to many people is frightening and unacceptable.

So we have to learn to cope with this new situation. You will need to examine the seeking, self-empowering aspect of yourself, as well as the 'need to sabotage' side that does not want these changes in your life and the responsibility that goes with them. So, watch for the saboteur!

That saboteur can be very convincing and will find many devices to slow you down or even stop you from succeeding. They include feelings of incredulity, impatience, having to deal with new conflicting emotions, new and different levels of fatigue, and so on.

One area where the saboteur can be really effective is in heightening the polarity between the right brain/imagination side of you and the left brain/logical, analytical side. Be aware of this struggle and always keep an open mind. Give credit to your discernment and scepticism, but do not allow either of them to control you. This open-mindedness can then enable you to see that sometimes your doubts are needed in order to slow you down, making your attempts to channel more steadily progressive.

Change on All Levels

It takes time for your personality and metabolism to cope with the subtle changes that developing as a channel can bring about. You could find that problems occur in your daily life and need attention. Quickening the vibration within you will bring disharmonies to the surface that will beg to be dealt with: they could be physical or emotional.

On a psychic level, it is also important that the transition is taking place at a comfortable pace and is not rushed or stressed. If psychic development takes place too quickly, it can cause energies to shoot up and down you out of control, creating an imbalance within your chakric system. It can also cause physical pain in the brow chakra for a period.

In fact, too much channelling too quickly can result in a state of psychic 'burn-out' which can be very debilitating on all levels.

113

It can affect the nervous system and cause nervous exhaustion, all of which will fuel the negative side of your doubts.

So take it gently, limiting yourself to once a week in the beginning. Then the many aspects of yourself will quicken gradually and harmoniously. Remember: 'When the pupil is ready, the door opens.'

Demanding Proof

There is also the side of you that demands proof and, if you have managed to establish communication with some form of guidance, may expect a miracle or an earth-shattering revelation every time you channel. True channelling is not like that. True channelling encourages the gentle emergence of your inner being and the creative side of you, sometimes bringing through a wisdom that lies beyond you.

A wonderful story is told of a very devout, religious man who found that his house was being threatened by floods. As the water reached the first floor, he prayed and said, 'Dear Lord, I have served and believed in you faithfully all my life, please protect and save me from this flood.'

At that moment, a motorboat appeared at the first-floor window and someone said, 'Hop in and we'll take you to safety.'

'No,' was the reply. 'I do not need you – the good Lord will save me.'

Still the flood waters rose and he clambered on the roof, holding on to a chimney. As he did so, a helicopter flew overhead and the pilot yelled out, 'Can I help you?'

'No,' said the devout man. 'I have led a good life and the good Lord will save me.' Five minutes later, the waters came over his head and he drowned.

When he reached the pearly gates he found, much to his surprise, that they were closed. 'What's going on?' he asked of God. 'I have been a good Christian all my life, been to church regularly and paid my taxes. Why did you not save me?'

God looked at him pityingly and said, 'I sent you a motorboat and a helicopter, but you turned me away!'

So you see, sometimes the simple message coming through another person is the way in which we are helped, and it can prove to be a revelation. Equally, the ego-motivated sense of importance will surely let you down. It is also true that both blind faith *and* demanding proof can lead us up the garden path, not only making us too blinkered to see properly, but allowing our ego to take over. We need to be unconditional and open-minded, yet disciplined in our approach.

Ego-based motivation in channelling can be highly dangerous, persuading us of an importance that is empty of true humility and understanding. As we know, like attracts like. So, following the maxim, the boosted ego of the channeller will attract an ego-orientated spirit, which in turn will pander to the ego of the listener. And that is the beginning of the downward slippery slope. You know the sort of thing: 'Do as I say and you will soon become a master, gain financially, be a great healer!'

It is by keeping open-minded yet questioning that we will find our balance as we progress, step by step.

Imagination?

We also need to deal with the argument: 'It's only my imagination.' So what if it is? What is your imagination? Albert Einstein, one of the world's greatest scientists said: 'Imagination is more important than knowledge.' It is through imagination that you can link to other levels of consciousness and other universes of experience. In fact, it is your imagination that enables you to become psychically aware and transcend matter; it is through your imagination that your spirit sometimes speaks. Just because you believe that your thoughts are merely reflecting your imagination does not mean to say that they are not valid.

Your doubts are important and they are trying to help you. Use

115

them as a positive, necessary force to motivate you to become a more discerning channel. Personally, I have had my share of doubts not only on the psychic level, but on a self-worth level as well. Today, I am exceedingly grateful for those doubts, for they have kept me on an even keel, enabling me to create a slowly-growing confidence in my channelling that I feel is not built on ego considerations. And I still have to be vigilant.

So, here's to your doubts!

A Journey into the Unknown

'H-A, everything I have been through in the last few weeks has made me feel, although quite wobbly, very strong and released, like a new beginning. You said before that it is good for us to be patient and listen, to love ourselves, need ourselves, be ourselves, and that fear of the forward movement will block our passage, or if we don't want to move forward we will be pulled back. I would like to move forward, I am fearful but I feel strong. If I follow your advice, will the answers come to me, because I don't want to make them up in my head?'

'I think deep down you know the route that you need to take. It is a route that is not easy because it is a journey into the unknown. You have found yourself in a position where you can no longer trust and that is very difficult. So you need to learn to trust yourself and your own inner responses. That can be your strongest and wisest guide.

'There are different roads you could take, and all represent different choices and opportunities. But you need to acknowledge the growth of your own empowerment and the continued blossoming forth of your own spiritual needs. And you have to build that into the future picture of what you would like your life to hold for you as you move forward. It must be built around those spiritual needs, *as a priority*. Once you have done that, the rest will fall into place.'

H-A (Gilly)

'You weave now a new fabric. Sometimes, when one weaves a new fabric, it means choosing a particular needle; and finding the appropriate needle for that fabric may take a little more time. But in the time of seeking for the needle, the pattern in the weaver's mind becomes a lot clearer. It is the space that allows the pattern to be thought through more clearly by the weaver.

'You are in that space, are you not, where you have the opportunity to think about how you would like your fabric to be, where you would like to place the light and the dark threads? For, without the dark threads you would not see the light, and vice versa. But when one jumps too quickly to form the pattern one can easily pick the wrong needle, and then the thread may be too coarse and it does not harmonise the colours.

'So, be in the space that allows the needle, the thread and the pattern to form in their own good time, and you will have worked with the essence of creation itself.

'It is the spirit of fire which allows inspiration to be grounded on the Earth plane from a powerful source. And as you know, fire can destroy; but when it destroys, it creates a fertile ground for more to grow on. You are in that process of destruction and re-creation. It is the space between destruction and re-creation that is important here, because it is about the birth of what is going to be created.

'Through that fire-inspiration can also come a clarity of vision, because fire helps the vision; it helps the passion of the soul to burn away, to be cleansed and then to see with a sharper vision.

'I wish to say this to each one here, that when the heat is great and intense and is burning away, these times allow for greater sharpness of vision. Those moments may be very

117

short, the vision intense. But be aware that this is in the air, it is around, that possibility of vision for each individual. Thank you for your question.

H-A (Gilly)

'Thank you.'

CHAPTER 13

Into the Future

*'You are indeed privileged to be incarnate at this great moment in
Earth's evolution, at this meeting point between the past and the
future; for this is the moment of a great shift in consciousness
marked by the transition from one solar age to the next.'*

H-A

As we reach and move beyond the millennium, we approach the
moment of transition into the Aquarian Age. For thousands of
years, the planet has been hampered by an overwhelming flow of
negative energy that has encouraged fear, guilt, the need for
personal power, the need for crime and retribution – qualities
that have made it difficult for the many positive aspects of the
human psyche to shine forth.

As I said earlier, we are just emerging from the Piscean Age in
which the expression of deep emotion has expressed itself vividly through the arts and creative achievements, but has been
overshadowed by the hierarchical, autocratic, rigid and personal
needs of the few. The over-riding question is: can the influences
of the Aquarian Age serve us any better?

As each age changes, there are opportunities for the planet to
recover its balance between the light and shadow of our evolution. We are told by H-A, who has helped many to find their own
levels of understanding, that recently the energies of light have
actually started to contain the Luciferian shadow aspects (in the
mythology of the planet, St Michael or Mikaal represents the
light and good, and Lucifer represents the shadow and evil), and
that we may look forward to an era in which humankind and all
associated forms of evolution will be able to move forward more
positively.

119

It must be remembered that the coming age is not a 'Golden Age', but merely a period in the history of the planet when different qualities will come to bear. It will be an age of the mind, self-empowerment and self-responsibility, decisions coming from consensus as opposed to dictatorship and, above all, the rise of people power. The prospects for this are exciting, but we will need to be aware of the possible chaos in establishing order and disciplines.

Channelling is a very Aquarian activity. I believe that it will gradually become a more intuitive activity, and that the ability to receive will become so natural and spontaneous that all channelling will become conscious and will be able to be used much more in many aspects of living. It will be more accessible, but also more challenging and more open to delusion; but I suppose that is the nature of humankind. Facing the duality of opportunity is the way we grow, and our ability to see ourselves as whole beings will provide stepping stones to rejoining and adding to the Godhead that created us. Despite the prognosis of the Prophets of Doom, I believe we are in an unequalled position to take ourselves into the future, becoming fuller and more fulfilled people.

'We have entered into an era of extremes: extremes of religion, extremes of politics, extremes of thinking; where science itself is beginning to look at areas of subtlety beyond those which would have been considered unprovable fifty years ago; where the Newtonian model is being usurped by much later paradigms that are adding emphasis towards this intuitive aspect of the human soul, so that humanity can bring through a strong spiritual awareness. Already it is starting to happen and I think it is important to emphasise that this modern approach to channelling is not something which has happened by chance. It is part of a process, an ongoing process which is going to extend further and further into human consciousness. So what I have been able to say through this sensitive and other sensitives is part of that picture.

120

'In front of us we have a fascinating future in which more and more people are starting to access these subtle levels of being in this way. I find it sad and disturbing that this more open and varied approach to spirituality should cause reactions within the Christian Church. I would dearly like to see the kind of inspiration that I am talking about, and that given by others like me, actually becoming part of the spiritual picture which emanates from the religious fraternity. It makes me feel sorrowful to see them stumbling on terms like "neo-paganism" and questioning how the country can progress with a diversity of spiritual thought. It is sad that they cannot see that the whole future of spiritual understanding on this planet lies in "unity in diversity", because this allows each individual to express their own understanding of universal belief. It is this very stuckness in the old ways of thinking that creates divisions, that creates polarity of thinking and behaviour.

'In my opinion, it is those who cling to those past traditions and attitudes who would destroy the very fabric of our society. If we are to find peace and goodwill, and unanimity of action towards that vision, it has to arise through honouring each other's beliefs, for when you condemn someone else, you condemn yourself.

'As we approach the festive season, this is a moment to look around with unconditional love and forgiveness. This is a time to honour the Christ consciousness. This is a time to honour and respect *all* beliefs.'

H-A in November 1996

'The world is facing an unequalled opportunity to find its redemption. Not a redemption based on any one God of any one religion, but redemption based on the universality of humankind's thinking.

'A school provides a preparation for stepping out into the exploration of adulthood and facing the exciting challenges that lie ahead. If humankind is to survive, these challenges need to be faced in a non-judgemental and open-minded way.

'We are entering an age in which each individual needs to acknowledge their responsibility to themselves and to every other form of life on this planet. With this kind of openness and respect, the future of humankind is unlimited. Without it, it is doomed – doomed by its own lack of vision and fear of moving from traditional viewpoints.

'Here's to the millennium and beyond!'

H-A

CHAPTER 14

H-A Answers Questions on Channelling

'I am what I am, no more and no less.'

H-A

The material from H-A in the first part of this chapter was channelled through me for a group of students.

'Good evening. I am here to answer your questions, but before the first question is asked, I would like to make a comment concerning channelling. A human being, as part of the evolution on this planet, is made up of various levels of consciousness – from the physical body, through the mental and emotional bodies, right through to the soul and the spirit, the latter being the created essence from God that motivates you. When you channel, you link all these levels of consciousness, from the physical *right through* to the spiritual, and beyond. It involves reaching within to your own levels of higher consciousness, the spiritual part of your divine being, and then moving beyond that to contact other levels of consciousness beyond yourself.

'I speak through this channel as a being of consciousness. For convenience you know me as "H-A" but I am an aspect of a group consciousness that has evolved beyond the need of physical incarnation, either through *Homo sapiens*, or through any other form of physical incarnation upon planet Earth.

'One of the benefits a spirit experiences through being

incarnate in a physical body is to be able to express spiritual understanding through the physical aspect of the emotions, for that is an experience that spirit cannot find in any other way.

'Channelling is about synthesising, bringing together, finding levels of harmony within your own being; and being able to use these levels of consciousness and communication to enhance every aspect of your physical life. It can enable your creativity to find new levels of expression; it will enable you to reach inside and find levels of empathy and understanding that you did not know you possessed. You are all children of God and channelling can help you to find that God within.

'Now I am here to answer your questions.'

'H-A, you actually answered in your opening one of the things I was going to ask you anyway, but perhaps you could go into a little more detail. The question is: "What processes are involved on the mental, emotional and physical levels, to make the conditions right to allow channelling to happen?"'

'It is like a beautiful, sensitive linking between each part of you, so that you find an inner harmony. Now this is not as simple as it sounds, because when you start to be in touch with each part of your being, and also increase the frequency of your psychic metabolism, each part of your being will start to be affected in the sense that it will quicken, and this may exaggerate certain attributes. On an emotional level, deep inner blockages may surface; if you have a health problem, it may become more obvious. It will make your digestive process more aware, more sensitive; it will make your breathing more sensitive; and you will become generally more aware of your body and its needs.

'One of the great advantages of working with the concept of channelling is that it offers you the opportunity of finding a greater measure of balance, of handling your life in a more positive way. It is like driving a sports car in which you can really feel the road beneath you. The challenging side of this is that you will no longer be able to cushion yourself from the things that you don't want to see and hear. And if you still persist in that, it will create problems for you. So it is heightening every aspect of your bodily existence and of your life.

'Channelling isn't necessarily about finding higher guides and great spiritual revelations. It can be, if that is your mission. But your mission may be to find ways of running your life that are more fulfilling. Maybe you write and wish to find more inspiration as a writer. Maybe you express your talents in some other way and would like to feel that the wheels are better oiled, thus using the process of channelling to improve your confidence and, consequently, your quality of life. The psychological effects of channelling are many and will reflect throughout your being.

'Thank you. I am ready for the next question.'

[*New questioner*]
'H-A, I wonder whether you could tell us the difference between channelling and guidance?'

'Channelling is about becoming more aware. Guidance is about using that awareness – to be able to recognise your personal guide and, maybe, other forms of guidance on other levels of existence.'

'Thank you. And how would you know in your daily life – because you've given a fairly broad definition of channelling – that you are channelling in a situation, for instance, if you are being creative, or if you're in the kitchen, or whatever you're doing? How can you know that you're actually channelling?'

'You need to study it, understand it and practise it; and through the awareness of that skill – because channelling is a skill – you are then able to bring it into your everyday living. It is done in a more conscious way.

'So when you come to cook your meal, you don't stand there

feeling irritable and angry. You simply stand there, relax and tune in, and you will suddenly find that what you are preparing will in itself take on a new dimension. Perhaps you will find you become more daring and make more use of herbs and spices. Maybe you will be inspired to produce meals in a way you have never produced them before. You know, perhaps I should promote this idea to cookery schools! [*chuckles*]'

'Are you saying then it's more a question of learning, practising and intent when one's doing something; because surely people can be channelling without realising it?'

'Of course . . .'

'When they're being creative . . .'

'Many people do channel without realising it. But as we move forward into this Aquarian Age, we are moving into an age of self-responsibility; and this means that, as you channel, it is important that *you are in charge* of that growth of awareness. Otherwise it will race away with you and you will be like a horse out of control. Maybe you will lose direction, maybe you will seek drugs or alcohol or some way of totally avoiding your own responsibilities in life. And you could easily disintegrate as a being.

'So it is no accident that this concept of channelling has surfaced. It has surfaced because it is a need of the age that we are moving into. And it is something everyone can benefit from. But it is important that *you are the boss*.

'Does that answer your question?'

'Just about, thank you. The only last thing I was thinking . . . does that imply that, as we move into the new age, people do need to learn from others about how to channel in order to bring it into their daily life; or is it a process which can happen on its own, as it were?'

'Like many things in life, my son, it is a process that can happen *totally naturally*, with the person being totally unaware of what is happening to them. But for some people, where the awareness is on a high level – and I use the word "high" in the sense of a quicker, finer frequency – there is the danger of going overboard if they are not in control and do not understand the rules.'

'Thank you. That does answer it.'

[*New questioner*]
'H-A, what is the experience like for you?'

'The experience, for me, is being part of a level of understanding that wishes to help the evolution of planet Earth in this time of transition.

'On a personal level, it is about identifying a spirit within a human body with whom I can relate, where there is a kind of *harmony* between us. Maybe on some level the channel and I have been together before. But I speak now, not as a human being, but as an essence from a group consciousness.

'So I have to bring myself, as it were, [*laughs*] down a funnel; I need to step down my normal frequency, because if I were to enter the sensitive bringing in the total energy of that frequency, I could shatter his physical body. I have to bring myself right down to a level whereby I can allow my consciousness to merge with his consciousness; and I try to do this as gently and smoothly as possible, for *his* sake.

'Remember, I am not the Ultimate God energy, and it is only on that Ultimate energy level that there is perfection; and *at any other level* there is no spirit with total, absolute wisdom. So I can err when I use the sensitive. I can put slightly too much energy in that can make him feel very exhausted at the end of the session; because instead of there being a harmonious link between us, it has become forced, tense, stressed, and that can put a strain on his nervous system and, for that matter, his whole body.

'So, for me, communicating through the sensitive has to be done with *great* sensitivity. I am also very mindful that I do not wish to use him in a way that would make him feel uncomfortable or frightened. It is for me like coming down a funnel in which the energy gets narrower and narrower and gentler and gentler. Often, I meet his spirit just outside his body because I know that he likes to come and meet me; and it is like bringing two currents together – two sounds together, until there is only one sound.

'The way in which I communicate through him is like some kind of telepathy; I use his brain, his mind and his being. It will have, therefore, partly *his* flavour. Over the years that we have been together we have learnt how to minimise this, so that our coming together can actually be a great joy. It is always a great joy for me to find someone who is incarnate on this Earth plane to be generous enough to allow me space; a space that I seek without a desire to control or to judge, but to support, to offer guidance, to answer questions and create concepts for you when you listen to me through that sensitive.

'How's that?'

'Wonderful, thank you.' [*Gentle laughter, then pause*]

[*New questioner*]
'H-A, does channelling always come from a more refined level of being?'

'No. It can be from any level of being.'

[*New questioner*]
'If somebody wishes to channel and to aspire to the higher levels, presumably the intent behind that motivation would assure that the more manipulative type of being does not come through to channel? Would that be correct?

'I do not believe that this is totally correct, for as well as good intent, it is important that the channeller carries out preparatory disciplines and also challenges whatever energies they feel around them. May I add that if there is an ego motivation, the channeller will draw ego-based energies towards them.

'The more your awareness grows, the more you shine like a beacon; for as you are having to face your own light and your own shadow, you can draw towards you both light and shadow.

'You may be fortunate, and you may be able to live all your life without encountering a shadow entity. But it can suddenly appear when you are least expecting it.

'You have heard me say on many occasions that the true path of spiritual awareness lies not in simply acknowledging the light, but in becoming a *whole* person; and becoming a whole person means that you are aware of every aspect of your being, of the light *and* the shadow, and that you are able to contain both and create a harmony and balance.

'Eventually, on this planet, the way to deal with the shadow will simply be through understanding it. At the moment it is dealt with on a rather more extreme tit-for-tat level. You know the expression: "If you live by the sword, you die by the sword." That message has been a prevailing one in the culture of this planet; and when people have tried to move beyond it – people like Gandhi, for example – they have created such a polarity that they have drawn the extreme negativity towards them. This is why Gandhi was assassinated. He was assassinated because the world wasn't ready for what he had to offer.

'As we move into the Aquarian Age, there will be opportunities to move beyond the need of the sword, which is one of the reasons why I am here speaking through this channel.

'Does that help?'

'Yes, I think so . . . to strive for the balance and to recognise and acknowledge both the light and the shadow. Thank you.'

[New questioner]
'H-A, it seems to me that if somebody were interested

in channelling, they would be taking a great risk because they would be allowing themselves to be extremely vulnerable to a spirit they can't choose, who may abuse their body, and if they haven't got a very healthy body, that might do them damage. I wonder what assurances one can actually gain – does one have to make sure that you learn channelling in a safe place?'

'The moment that you entered your physical body within the womb of your mother, your whole being was at risk. From the moment that you were born into the world from the womb of your mother, your whole life was at risk. Every time that you cross a busy main road, your life is at risk. I do not consider that learning how to channel is any more risky than any other occupation on your planet.

'If you climb into a fast sports car and drive it very fast before you have learnt how to drive and before you have read your Highway Code, you will very likely end up not only hurting yourself but somebody else.

'As a teacher, I feel that I would be falling short if I were not to point out that channelling, like anything else in life, poses challenges. But equally, I can assure you that if you go about it in a clear, balanced and controlled way, your fears will be minimal. The risks of coming to a sticky end will be minimal. You could say, my child, that it is less risky than the job that you do at the moment.' [*Laughter all round*]

'That I believe.' [*Laughter*]

'I hope that assures you.'

'Oh, thank you. I'll learn the Highway Code.' [*More laughter*]

[*New questioner*]
'H-A, could you possibly tell us whether you know the other guides working through sensitives? We know

them by names, perhaps. Could you say how you relate to or understand the other energies who are working through other sensitives at this time from the same sort of level?'

'I see us as being different flavours of the same fruit, meeting the needs and the readiness of the sensitives with whom we associate. So, for example, if a level of consciousness from my own group wished to speak through you, they would match whatever it is that you felt you had to offer and, in making that match, they would synthesise with your own consciousness, and move forward.

'In the group that I have worked with, I have offered my own consciousness level to a number of sensitives. If they choose to use that frequency and synchronise with it – fine. If they feel that they want to move towards something that is more akin to their own consciousness – fine.

'A very typical example of this is Diane, who brings through a guidance that calls itself "Lama". Now, Lama and I are from the same level of consciousness; Lama is the *yin* and I am the *yang* expression of this consciousness. We therefore blend together very well and we make a whole when we associate and channel together at the same time. But I know that the *yang* aspect suits this sensitive and the *yin* aspect suits Diane. This is nothing to do with either the physical sex or the personality of the two channellers; it is much more to do with the actual spirit that is inside the physical body of Tony and the spirit within the physical body of Diane.

'Have I answered your question adequately?'

'I think so, because I'm not quite sure what kind of answer I was looking for.' [*Laughter*]

'And I was not sure what kind of answer you were looking for. So I chose one that I thought would be appropriate.' [*Laughter*]

'In a way, I was trying to get a clearer idea of how you identify at your level of consciousness with other

131

**beings at the same level, and I think you answered it
fairly well . . .'**

'Where there is what I call "teaching" going on – and I come
from a teaching level, you understand – there are many spirits
who incarnate with the mission of allowing themselves to
associate with us, because even in channelling it needs collusion
on both sides. So, my need meets Tony's need and Tony's need
meets my need. So we become as one; and he chose this life so
that this would be part of his process.

'He might have chosen to work with spirits of departed souls –
in other words, people who have recently left physical
incarnation; and, from my perspective, that kind of work is just
as important. So he would have attracted a very different type of
spirit towards him. Are we not all part of the whole?

'There you are – a bonus on the original answer!'

'Thank you.'

[New questioner]
**'I have a question. I feel that often, in my work – and
I'm not aware of it until later when I look back – I
think, "That came from somewhere else, rather than
from me." I'd like to know if I could actually channel
consciously and use it for the benefit of what I'm
doing.'**

'If I may be permitted to correct you on one thing: you are
already using it as a benefit for what you are doing. The only
answer that I can offer you is "with practice", with setting out to
be aware – perhaps by finding someone to work with who will
help and ask the right questions for you when you are trying to
channel.

'So the effort for that would have to come from you. But of
course it would be supported by us. I feel I can put this to you in
this way because you are already well down the road and you
understand what I am talking about. Your awareness is working

on a level in which you know that you've been aware, even if it has not happened spontaneously at the time. So your problem is how to be aware of being aware; and the answer is to work with someone or some group that can guide you.'

'Have you any suggestions on the last point?'

'I think the choice of that would have to come from yourself.'

'Thank you.'

'I'm not dodging the answer there; I'm actually answering it. Where this type of development is concerned – and you have come into this body with a spiritual motivation, you understand that, don't you? – the choice has to be yours. But is it so difficult a choice? Are there not those amongst your friends to whom you could go and ask the same question?'

'There are quite a few.'

'And maybe, my dear, you need to experiment a little – Hmm? The whole exciting thing about expanding your awareness is that there is no right or wrong way of going about it; and that all experience is valid. So what is important, when one is within a physical body, is to say to oneself, "I am going to put my foot into the water to test the temperature. And if the temperature in *this* pool is not to my liking, I will go to the next pool and try that one, until I find a pool that feels right." And then, when that happens, the doors will open.'

'Thank you.'

[*New questioner*]
'So are you talking about different ways of channelling – when someone consciously channels, and when someone channels quite naturally, because of their own . . .?

'I answered the previous questioner in a way that I felt was applicable for her. But if I were going to generalise the question more, of course there is no right answer. In other words, for some people spontaneous channelling on a certain level maybe adequate and safe and OK and will happen for them anyway.

'What I have been talking about this evening is for those people who are saying, "I want to improve my level of awareness. I am no longer content with what I already have." Does that help?'

'I'm not sure. The reason I'm asking you is because once I had a session of channelling and it felt really uncomfortable – not going out of my body, but actually coming back into it. So channelling in that way didn't feel right for me. But I know that at other times I feel as if I'm channelling quite naturally.'

'Maybe your channelling comes through your pen. Channelling does not necessarily mean doing what I am doing through this channel.'

'Right – that's what I'm asking you.'

'Channelling can be about just improving your awareness of whatever it is that you are doing in your life.'

[*New questioner*]
'So it's where your focus is.'

'It is where you are focusing, and it is a very important aspect as we go into the Aquarian Age and I would like to explain why. Because we are going into an age in which the accent will be on the mind and mental things, it is really quite important that people start to find ways of actually developing that awareness side.

'In the Piscean Age, channelling has been quite prevalent, although in a very unconscious way: you've had all the great painters, artists and composers, architects, and so on. Some of the great scientists, politicians, inventors and businessmen have all been channels, many of them *totally* unaware of it. But somehow that suited the atmosphere of the Piscean Age.

'As we enter this Aquarian Age, everything is going to be very much more mindful; it is a different ball game. This is an age which, if people are not prepared to work on opening their consciousness, could become a very destructive age. It could become an age in which feelings and emotions are totally ignored. I don't think I need to go into what that could entail. But it could be very frightening.

'Let me remind you that this coming Aquarian Age will not be a *golden* age; it is merely a time when the accent will be different, in which the potential and the opportunities will be immense. I am not a prophet of doom; I admire and respect the tremendous overall efforts that humankind has made in the past fifty years. There are still wars and torture and pestilence, because the human race and indeed the entire planet has not yet reached that stage when it can do without them. This is a part of the process of evolution of the planet.

'Yes, of course, channelling can be so spontaneous that the recipient is not even aware that they are channelling. But in the Aquarian Age that could be more dangerous. So I believe that as we go forward, this understanding of being prepared to be *in charge of your awareness* is important.

'Thank you for your question which enabled me to give that answer. Are there any other aspects of channelling which I have not covered that you would like me to speak on?'

[*New questioner*]
'H-A. I'd like to ask, "How much are you influenced by the sensitive that you're coming through?"'

'If I may give you a humorous answer, my son, I would say, "It depends on the weather."' [*Laughter and giggles*]

'I was just thinking that you have quite a strong sense of identity when you come through the sensitive. Do you have an individual identity as well as being an aspect of group consciousness?'

'I think the easiest way to answer your question is to say, "Have you heard me speaking through another sensitive?"'

'Yes.'

'And how did that feel to you?'

'It felt the same. I could sense your energy . . . strong.'

'Then maybe one day you'll allow me to speak through you.'

'I hope so.'

'In merging with the consciousness of a human being, there are all kinds of, if I may use a popular expression, "hidden agendas". How do I manage when I'm trying to convey something through the sensitive that he doesn't want to hear? How do I cope when there is something I want to convey through the sensitive that his brain does not seem capable of understanding?

'The relationship has to be very subtle, very gentle. But instances can happen when I wish to convey something that is very much against his own beliefs – and we do have variances, believe me.

'So it is about a working relationship, you're quite right about that; and some concepts are easier for me to convey through *this* particular sensitive than others. When I speak through Gilly Wilmot, for example, I am able to convey things through her sometimes that I am not able to convey through this sensitive, and vice versa.

'So from my point of view, it is a very privileged position to be able to speak through more than one sensitive, and important too. Just think of the profound effect that the Tibetan had, being able to speak through Alice Bailey as well as Madame Blavatsky.

'I think it is important for any energy, any "-ology", if you like – can I use the word "-ology"? – I think it is important for any "-ology" to be *open* to moving forward; and that means *it must always be ready to receive and engender new ideas.* Indeed, I am able to say things through this sensitive tonight that I could not have said forty years ago, because he has changed and I have changed, and the nature of our liaison has changed. Probably, after he and I decide that we have had enough in this life, I will be able to speak through other channels who will pick up where we, as a partnership, have left off. Because, for me, *spiritual understanding is an ongoing process*, and I hope and pray that the major religions are really going to open their hearts and minds to this understanding. If they don't, they will crumble. And that is a prophecy.

'That has probably gone a little further than you bargained for when you asked your question.'

'Thank you.'

[*New questioner*]
'H-A, I have a question. It is about resolving the conflict between wanting to be open to channelling but fearing it, thinking that I can't do it and that I'm blocking it.'

'I think you have to honour and be very thankful and joyous for the side of you that thinks you are not good enough to do it. That is the quality that will help to ensure that you are really aware of what you are doing and will take each step slowly and carefully, not falling into the trap of allowing your own ego to take over.

'So the best advice that I can give you is to honour and to nurture that side of you that is sceptical of your own ability. If it is your wish to channel, then it is my belief that you are capable of doing so on a level that is right for you; and you are the only person who can find out what that level is.

'Thank you.'

[*New questioner*]
'H-A. I have a couple of questions I'd like to ask, and one is "When one comes to communicate with you

**through the channel, it has very much a ring or sense
of what it must have been like in the past to have
consulted the oracle; and I was wondering whether you
could say something about the difference between
times of old, when people would consult the oracle,
and channelling today, as we are witnessing it now?"'**

'You know, on one level, the difference is very much less than you
may think. One of the difficulties, if you are speaking of the
Greek oracle such as at Delphi – one of the difficulties was the
people who ran it, who had political agendas, who wanted to
hold control and say, "We will interpret what comes through the
channel . . ." It hasn't changed very much, has it?!' [*Laughter*]

**'Is that a personal comment? [*Laughter*] You mean the
interpretation?'**

'Of course.'

**'I think it has actually. What I was meaning was that
people would go to the oracle without acknowledging
their own ability to be open to their own insight and
what . . .'**

'Because that followed, my son, the hierarchical energy of the
previous ages, where everything had to be controlled from some
kind of higher source; and here, of course, we're hitting again
the basic difference of moving into the Aquarian Age when,
once more, humankind has the opportunity of breaking out of
that fear-ridden kind of autocratic, dominating management of
the planet.

'We are truly moving into an era of individual responsibility,
individual empowerment, individual understanding. It isn't
going to be easy because the very process of trying to make a
change like that is going to bring up a lot of problems and
difficulties. Many people will not want it, for it means that no
longer can you go to the "oracle", the higher authority, and get
some kind of answer to your question.

'It means you've got to work it out for yourself. And, indeed, what I have attempted to do this evening is to stir your imagination and your creativity, to enable you to decide what you could do about your need to expand your consciousness. I haven't told you how to do it because that needs to be your choice. You have already started through what you call your "School of Channelling"; and I think this has already opened up centres within you, has it not? You have the choice of going further along those lines, or, again, striking out in some other direction. If you still wish to work with us, then you can channel aspects of this level of consciousness. This applies to a number of you in this room.

'But the age that we are moving into is not about creating guruship, mastership, or any form of superiority where the power is centred in the hands of a few. It really and truly is about *unity in diversity*; it is allowing the individual to find God within, rather than God without. So the choices are infinite, are they not? Thank you.'

'Thank you.'

[New questioner]
'H-A, you say that you are here and you have no wish to manipulate. But from one point of view, talking and teaching in this way can alter the future by changing our approach to the world, and could also be seen as a form of manipulation on a much larger scale . . .'

'I understand that. But I do not compel you to follow any aspect of my teaching. I do not threaten you with emotional blackmail of what will happen if you do not follow an aspect of my teaching. It is given as a free will offering that you can accept or reject on any level.

'Of course there will be those who will try to accuse me of manipulation. I can only speak from my centre of understanding; and I know, from the level of consciousness from which I speak, there is no deliberate, conscious intention of

139

manipulation – and even the sensitive is allowing me to say that through him.' [*Chuckles*]

'But if you change, inadvertently maybe, change the future . . .'

'I am not here to change the future; I am here to say to you that, if it is your wish to hear what I am saying and you feel that that *resonates* with your own *raison d'être*, then it is your own choice if you want to affect the future of the planet by what you have found and learnt. But in affecting the future of the planet, I would like to say to you, I hope you will do it as an offering, not as a manipulation.

'There are many aspects of what I'm teaching that I understand and realise are radical; and because of the radical nature of what I'm saying, I am opening my teaching to abuse, I am opening myself to abuse and, sadly, I am probably opening the sensitive to abuse. But that is the nature of evolution and, at the end of the day, truth can only be an offering – never a rule, never a law, and never a "must". That is the best I can offer you.'

'Thank you.'

'The trust that you have to place in me is that I do not see this as a glorious opportunity to influence the future of the world. Because the moment that I believed I was here to change the future of the world, my teaching would be in great trouble, morally and ethically.

'I have not come to save the world. I have come to offer a greater understanding that hopefully will enable those thereon to find their way forward with greater vision – without judgement, without manipulation and without condition.

'Thank you.'

[*New questioner*]
'H-A, a few years ago I used to wonder why through channelling we couldn't just be given all of the technological breakthroughs we need to help the

planet. I've since realised that that would just be treating the symptoms and not the cause and that our spiritual development is really the key.'

'It would also, my son, if I may say so, be like giving a nuclear bomb to a child of three to play with.'

'Recently, though, I was reading one of your teachings from 1985 and it talked about the cooperation between entities, spirit consciousnesses from other planets. It talked about higher consciousnesses incarnating into physical bodies from other more highly developed planets . . .'

'I would not retract any of that, my son. If the planet collectively chooses to accept the opportunities of a transit from one age to another, to take a tangible step forward in its evolution, it will need people – bodies – to work through. Even Jesus needed the body of the Christ . . . I think the sensitive has inverted my words there . . .' [*Laughter*]

'When the Christ energy was offered to the planet, it needed a body to manifest through, and it had Jesus, the man. In my understanding, there are many souls on this planet, in male bodies and female bodies, who have chosen this time to incarnate, to allow spirits into those physical bodies so as to offer guidance to enable the planet to move forward.

'I would like to make one thing clear, which is, I know, a divergence from what other channels have said: when a spirit enters the body at the moment of conception, this is a perfectly natural process, and the energies of God like to work within a natural process. In my understanding, it is very rare for a spirit to take over a developed body. If and when this does happen, I would be most concerned as to the wisdom of such an action. You understand what I'm saying here? I know that I am cutting across what has been said elsewhere, but I think it is really important to understand that the manifestations of the universe work best in harmony with natural processes. They do not work through manipulated processes. If they *are* working through manipulated processes, then I think one would always need to be very aware of the type of energy involved.

'OK?'

'Hm. Thank you.'

'The energy is dropping a little and, before the sensitive inverts anything else that I say, is there perhaps one last question – a quickie?'

[*New questioner*]
'Perhaps just a comment from yourself on the title of the book about to be published – maybe it would be interesting for the sensitive to hear your point of view.'

'It is the sensitive's book – not mine.'

'Wasn't it inspired by you at all then?'

'It was his choice. [*Laughter*]

'May I thank you, each and every one, for asking your questions; and if you haven't asked any questions, may I thank you for *just being here*, for it has been a privilege to work with this group tonight. The energies have felt positive and I thank you for all that you have given. Good night and my blessings.'

[*All*] **'Goodnight.'**

The following session, in which H-A was channelled through both myself and Gilly Wilmot, was given at the end of a two-day workshop on channelling. I have indicated where Gilly acted as the channel.

'Before answering your questions, I would like to express a few words on the subject of freedom.

'This has been two days of discovery, two days of finding freedom. Remember, my friends, that freedom is a state of mind, not a state of being: freedom from fear, freedom from tradition, from being encased in rigidity. And freedom from not being able to see the road to take.

'Maybe the last freedom is the easiest to answer, for it is about understanding that when we are in touch with that spiritual impulse within, we no longer need to look ahead anxiously; because we have found a resonance with the innermost part of our being and we know that the road will be revealed to us. It is also the only way to move ahead. It means moving beyond the personal self, beyond the needs of the ego, beyond the need of compulsion. It means finding freedom.

'This freedom is a gift that every spirit has within its grasp because it is a state of mind which is totally independent of your circumstances, of your situation, of your life. It is something that is totally free of whatever prison you have created for yourself. It means that you can allow your spirit to soar into the sky and explore the heavenly realms, the realms that are your rightful heritage.

'Each one of you has chosen this life in a very special way. Each one of you chose to come together during these two days, for you each have something to teach the other. So, I say to you, be patient, be loving, be yourself.

'You are incarnate at a very important time in the history of the planet. A time when the forces of light have assembled in such a way that they are challenging the forces of darkness; where light and shadow are showing themselves to each other. We need to blend those two energies and not allow them to face each other in confrontation. It is a time for understanding and forgiveness and always moving on, moving beyond the fear of moving on; because when that fear begins to present itself, your left brain will gather up its arms and will find every conceivable reason why you should not move on: "It will push you across safe boundaries", "Better the devil you know than the devil you don't." And yet, dear friends, there is always something breathtaking, exciting around that next corner.

'However, you can only look around that next corner when you can truly say to yourself, "I have dealt with the past".

Dealing with the past does not mean acquiescing to it, it does not mean that you have in one flick of the fingers pushed the past away, throwing it across the room. It is about understanding that all that past heritage is important because it is making you what you are *now*, today, at this moment in time. Dealing with the past is being able to look back at that past with gratitude and saying, "The compassion that I have now, the understanding that I have now, is because of the suffering I allowed myself to go through, that I *needed* to go through in the past. I understand that in letting go of it I have cut the chains; but it is still there and I need it to be there because it is the fertiliser of my future. It is that part of my consciousness that is enabling me to move forward.'

'So, in releasing the past, letting go of it, you are not – if I may use one of your Earth expressions that seems most appropriate – you are not throwing the baby out with the bathwater. You are just letting go, you are cutting the chains where they have so successfully sabotaged you that they have drawn you into a nervous wreck and racked your body with pain. Where they have made you unable to support yourself on your legs and even made your body erupt in protest. Where they have blinded you to reality and have surrounded you with a tradition that threatens your very creativity. Where the very pain of the past makes it difficult for you to breathe into the future.

'So dear friends, hear me, for I have tried to strike a chord that will resonate within each one of you to help you to understand what precious spirits you are. How very special you each are, how very special every soul is; each one of you has so much to offer, not only to others but to yourself. For within each physical body beats a heart that cares, a heart that has the capacity to reach out in forgiveness, in compassion, and in a love that is untainted by ego. You know what I mean by that, don't you? For when love becomes tainted by ego it becomes very conditional and it is built all around by what other people are going to think of you, how other people are going to judge you, and words like "obligation" begin to creep in and infiltrate and sabotage most viciously and successfully. So this is a plea for you to listen to yourselves, to love yourselves and to need yourselves, for as we look to tomorrow we can see that there are challenges that face us. But in helping ourselves we will be able to face these challenges; and through facing our own challenges, we will be able to help others.

'I am here to answer your questions through either Gilly or Tony or both. So perhaps I should put it into the royal "we" and say we await your first question.'

'H-A, the last time we spoke you gave me a reference. I quote: "Make a leap even before you look. Place all momentous thoughts in small hands, their strength lies in their wisdom which is heaven sent." How do I recognise this, because at present I can't?'

'What is it you wish to recognise, my son?'

'Well, just in what direction do these small hands move and where is their strength?'

'You are as strong as you wish to be. And there are many small hands of guidance around you. I want to say to you to cast away your fears, your fears of being imperfect. Cast away your fears of "not being able to" and face your life fairly and squarely. Ask yourself what you need to do with your life that will bring you fulfilment. Ask yourself where your heart lies, for in your heart is the truth. In your heart is the inner motivation of your own divine being. *In your heart* is the direction in which you need to go, the acknowledgement of where you are in your life and what you have achieved in it. *In your heart* lies your next step forward. *In your heart* lies the need to grow beyond the fear of stepping outside the demands of society and the culture in which you have lived.

'I think I have given you a great deal to think about there . . . and I would like to use the other sensitive to bring out another aspect, so just allow me to switch.'

'You speak of recognition my friend, of being unable to recognise that which is so close to you. By what means do you recognise a person? I Ask you a question on this physical plane, think about it. How do you recognise another human being who comes into the same space as yours? Hm?' (H-A, Gilly)

'I live with her and we work together as a team.'

'I do not talk of the person who lives with you; perhaps I need to say a person whom you have previously seen, who enters your sphere. Let us keep it a little outside the family. What do you do? How do you recognise them? Do you touch them? Do you see them?' (H-A, Gilly)

'Yes, I do indeed, and I converse with them.'

'You converse with them. You find a point of common interest between you, something that joins you together, something that enables you to say we are both human beings together, yes?' (H-A, Gilly)

'Yes.'

'So when it comes to recognition of the subtler levels around you, you can employ just the same ways; but listen, look and feel from a different level, from a different perspective. Find the resonance, that which is in common so that you can build a relationship thereon. And it is indeed recognising from the level of the heart, not from the level of the thinking-mind, but from the level of the heart-mind, which sees, which hears, which experiences, which touches with a completely different quality, another sense. Allow yourself to open, to resonate with what is around you at this moment, see what you can recognise with the heart-mind, not the head-mind. Can you do that?' (H-A, Gilly)

'I will try to do that and I think I understand you. Thank you.'

'You have another question?' (H-A, Gilly)

'Well, the other question is about relived experiences. Are these relived in different circumstances, at

146

different times, to test the spirit's choice in such
matters or do some spirits meet and work again
together to unravel their answers?'

'Yes.' [*Silence and laughter*]

'They do meet again, I take it?'

'Of course.'

'If you had a puzzle you wished to solve lying on your table,
you would come to it again and again, would you not, before you
felt that the pieces fitted together. Hm?'   (H-A, Gilly)

'Yes.'

'So in that sense it is the same; you may wish to return to an
experience time and time again to bring the balance, to bring the
puzzle into a picture that can be looked at from an altogether
different perspective. But you are also within the picture. So it
means two levels of awareness.

'It would help you my friend, if you could also consider two
levels of awareness within yourself. You are in the middle of an
experience, allowing everything to be as it is. But on another
level, you are, as it were, on your own shoulder, aware of what is
happening. It is rather like being in a state of meditation when
doing the dishes or walking the dog. You know that you are in the
three-dimensional world, but you keep a door subtly open to
connect with spirit, you keep a pathway along which the higher
levels of expression can inspire, nourish and guide; and that door
is gently open to allow the flow.

'I felt I wanted to say that to you as perhaps a way to connect
with that which you feel eludes you.'   (H-A, Gilly)

'Thank you. Yes, I understand.'

[*New questioner*]
**'H-A, may I ask a question. There are situations when
your heart takes you one way and perhaps your mind**

another. You feel you are doing the right thing but inevitably, at a certain point, fences have to be erected in order to avoid hurting others. Therefore, you are left on one side of the fence because of that possible hurt, generally alone, and this can stretch through the years and become a burden. You feel you made the right choice but in some cases it could be wrong. So, what do you do about it?'

'My child, there is no such thing as a right or wrong choice; there is only the choice that you choose. So it is for me about acceptance and forgiveness.'

'Would you wear all the clothes all your life from your childhood? Would you keep wearing the many layers of your clothes all at once?' (H-A, Gilly)

'No.'

'Would you carry all of the baggage?' (H-A, Gilly)

'No. Preferably not.'

'And yet you choose to carry these many layers, do you not? You seem loath to let them go. You still carry baggage from previous journeys that weighs you down; and if you are weighed down, you cannot come to that lightness of being that you so dearly wish. While you look back you can never see the road ahead. It is where your focus is. There is no conundrum as I would understand it. Indeed, it is simple.' (H-A, Gilly)

'I see it as if I have left a great deal of baggage behind. The road ahead in certain directions I do see very clearly, but there is always the danger . . . I mean, one wouldn't hurt animals and one tries not to hurt people, so inevitably there can only be a certain line of conduct. I would see it as a sort of fence where you don't go over the fence. Or if you do give out an intensity of caring which goes beyond the fence . . . it

is going to reverberate on somebody else and hurt them.'

'Then you are sitting on the fence in bondage, my friend.'
(H-A, Gilly)

'Yes.'

'When you walk outside this building and walk upon the path, what do you walk upon?'
(H-A, Gilly)

'Preferably green grass.'

'And what lives within the green grass, amongst the fine blades of green grass, what lives there?'
(H-A, Gilly)

'Earth and little animals.'

'Hm. And some of these little animals are very tiny, so what do you think happens as you walk upon the green grass?'
(H-A, Gilly)

'You crush them to death.'

'Yes.'
(H-A, Gilly)

'Which has been one of my . . . well, I don't really like killing spiders, it has been one of my rules to try not to damage . . .'

'Can you see what I am saying to you? That, if you take a step, then you are creating movement. You may create a form of destruction as you would when you tread on the grass; but, if you do not act, then you are forever in this state, aren't you? You are forever impaled, bound on the fence.'
(H-A, Gilly)

'Yes.'

'You can only be what you are and allow that to shine forth through you. You cannot be all things to all beings; you can only be true to yourself and then you will be true to other beings.'

149

'As Shakespeare said, "To thine own self be true, and it must follow, as the night the day, thou canst not then be false to any man" . . . Thank you, H-A.'

'I think we have reached a moment when we need to leave the sensitives, but we hope that, in what we have said, we have given answers and challenged some situations for each one of you. We love you and we thank you for allowing us to be with you.'

[*Together*] **'Thank you, H-A, our love to you.'**

The School
of Channelling

Today, there are a number of schools and colleges offering guidance and tuition to people who wish to develop as healers. But there is little help on an organised scale for those who recognise that they have intuitive gifts which they would like to develop in a structured, sequential and safely contained way.

The School of Channelling (see p. 153 for address) has been set up for those who would like to explore their intuition or psychic sensitivity in a series of carefully constructed weekend workshops, rather than attending a group on a weekly basis. The school acknowledges channelling in its broadest form, as a way for people to connect consciously with their inspirational levels, enhancing the expression of their creativity.

Each of the three workshops is part of a sequence, offering practical guidance on how to handle and ground psychic energy safely, and enabling you to acknowledge the extent and direction of your psychic potential. We believe that the ratio of tutor to students is important, and in any experiential work on channelling we ensure that there is one tutor for every six students. After the workshop, every student receives personal sponsorship and supervision, and peer support is organised, i.e. students are put in touch with other students with whom they can practise.

When the three-part course is completed, we offer ongoing development groups so that there are always opportunities for further guidance and support.

Bibliography and Further Reading

Benson, Herbert, MD, *Your Maximum Mind*, Aquarian Press, 1988

Bloom, William, *Psychic Protection*, Piatkus, 1996

Cirlot, J. E., *A Dictionary of Symbols*, Routledge and Kegan Paul, 1962

Eastcott, Michael J., *The Silent Path*, Rider, 1969

Furlong, David, *Develop Your Intuition and Psychic Powers*, Bloomsbury, 1996

Hope, Murry, *Practical Techniques of Psychic Self-Defence*, HarperCollins, 1983

Hope, Murry and Ann Neate, *Meditations*, The Atlanteans, 1980

Klimo, Jon, *Channelling*, Aquarian Press, 1988

Perls, Fritz, *The Gestalt Approach and Eye Witness to Therapy*, Bantam, 1976

Roman, Sanaya and Duane Packer, *Opening to Channel*, H. J. Kramer Inc., 1987

Swainson, W. P., *Three Famous Mystics – Swedenborg*, Rider, nd

Weigell, Arthur, *The Life and Times of Akhnaton*, Thornton Butterworth, 1922

White, Ruth, *Working with Your Chakras*, Piatkus, 1993

Williamson, Linda, *Contacting the Spirit World*, Piatkus, 1996

Wilson, Annie, *Where There's Love*, Gateway, 1986

Useful Addresses

Organisations and people to contact if you wish to attend courses or need advice or help

School of Channelling, Runnings Park, Croft Bank,
West Malvern WR14 4DU
Tel: 01684 573868 Fax: 01684 892047

College of Healing
Also at Runnings Park (see above)

College of Psychic Studies, 16 Queensberry Place,
London SW7 2EB
Tel: 0171 589 3292

Ruth White, Dragons Den, 3 Manor Farm Mews,
Tidmarsh RG8 8EY
Tel: 01734 845480

Atlanta Association, 33 Beacon Hill Court, Wood Road,
Beacon Hill, Hindhead GU26 6PU
Tel: 01428 605412

Hertha Larive
(Advice and help only)
Tel: 01865 730486

Index

Index

Index

Index

Index

Smith, Joseph, 14
smoking, 79
Society of Friends, 14
Socrates, 13
solar ages, 13
solar plexus chakra, 51
soul, 47
Sperry, Dr R.W., 18–19
spirit, 45–6, 48
  'astral travel', 106
  and aura, 32
  and death, 97
  Higher Self, 28, 96
  meditation, 58
  returning to body, 41–4
spirit-delusion, 29
spiritual crises, viii–ix
spiritual mission, 110–11
spiritual realms, 98
spiritualism, 14–15
Steiner, Rudolf, 16
stroking the aura, 53
'stuckness', 66, 110, 121
subtle bodies, 46–8, 50, 52
Swainson, W.P., 14
Swedenborg, Emanuel, 14
symbols:
  centring, 44
  clairvoyance, 25
  psychic protection, 70–4

Taillard, René, 4–5
technology, 140–1
Theosophical Society, 15
'third eye', 47
throat chakra, 50

trances, 4
  oracles, 12
transformative journey, xi
truth, absolute, 94–5

ultimate truth, 95
unconscious channelling, 28
unconscious mind, 105
universal rhythms, 109–10
universe, 8
universe of energy, 102

values, 109
visualisation, meditation, 59, 60,
  62–4
vitamin B complex, 80

water:
  drinking, 78, 86
  element, 63–4
White Cloud, 5–6
White Eagle, 8, 16
White Lodge, 16
Wilmot, Gilly, xi–xiv, 136, 142
Witchcraft Act, 5
Wrekin Trust, 9
writers' block, 104
writing:
  automatic, xi–x
  creativity, 100

yin and yang:
  energy, 19–21
  symbol, 74

zodiac, 13